BLACKOUT LOOTING!

BLACKOUT LOOTING!

NEW YORK CITY, JULY 13, 1977

By ROBERT CURVIN and BRUCE PORTER

Foreword by Mitchell Sviridoff
for the Ford Foundation

GARDNER PRESS, INC., New York
Distributed by Halsted Press
Division of John Wiley & Sons, Inc.
New York   London   Toronto   Sydney

The names of most individuals men-
tioned in this work, except those of public
officials, have been changed. Also, the
identity of some locales has been altered.

GARDNER PRESS, INC.
19 Union Square West
New York 10003

Distributed solely by the Halsted Press Division
of John Wiley & Sons, Inc., New York

Library of Congress Cataloging in Publication
Data

Curvin, Robert.
Blackout looting, New York City, July 13, 1977.

Bibliography: p.
1. Robbery—New York (City)
2. Pillage—New York (City)
3. Criminal justice, Administration of—New
York (City)
I. Porter, Bruce, joint author.   II. Title.
HV6661.N7C87   364.1'55   78-20817
ISBN 0-470-26627-9 (paper)
ISBN 0-470-26669-4 (cloth)

DESIGNED BY SIDNEY SOLOMON

Printed in the United States of America

For
Patricia Curvin
and
Lorna Scott Porter

CONTENTS

FOREWORD

In the wake of the widespread looting during the July 13, 1977, blackout in New York, much instant analysis found its way into the newspapers, magazines and the electronic media about why it happened, whose fault it was and how best to prevent recurrences. The information on which such analysis was based was gathered in a hurry, and interpretation often followed predictable lines. Some saw the events as the product of bad social and economic conditions in the ghettoes and blamed the society as a whole. Others wrote or spoke of the erosion of a sense of right and wrong, of respect for property, and of the need for national and civic leadership to face up to these problems.

We at the Foundation were unwilling to accept any single interpretations because experience has taught us that contemporary urban problems do not lend themselves to simple or ideologically consistent explanations. But we did feel that the

ix

events of the night of the 1977 blackout had something to teach us. To learn it, we needed to move while the data were fresh and the people who had been involved—whether in looting, as victims, or on the law enforcement and administrative sides—were available and their memories accurate.

Robert Curvin and Bruce Porter were well qualified to do the job. Mr. Curvin has had a distinguished career in community organization, and as an author and scholar on urban affairs. Mr. Porter has a fine record as a journalist, with extensive experience in covering urban affairs and analyzing social issues.

The two authors proceeded to cull systematically the records of key municipal departments and agencies and to do extensive interviewing of people in all the areas where looting had occurred. What they found gives us new information and insights about the motivation of the looters, the strategy of and the constraints on law enforcement agencies, the wide geographic dispersion of the poverty population in New York City, the extent to which there is a relationship of looting to employment, economic condition and aspiration, and about other aspects of the attitudes and values that shape events and life in some of New York City's communities.

Because the work of Curvin and Porter adds to our knowledge and serves to refine our judgment, I believe it is of value and the Foundation is pleased to have sponsored it.

Mitchell Sviridoff
VICE PRESIDENT
FORD FOUNDATION

ACKNOWLEDGMENTS

This book is a result of research commissioned by the Ford Foundation. Our work could not have been done without its financial and logistical backing. It also could not have been accomplished without the help of numerous public officials, including former Police Commissioner Michael Codd; his former Chief of Operations, James F. Hannon, Fire Commissioner John T. O'Hagan; his Chief of Planning and Operations Research, Ronald Browne; Charles Kuhlman of the New York City Criminal Justice Agency; Marilyn Burkehardt of the New York City Planning Commission; its former chairman, Victor Marrero, and the numerous people who shared their experience on the night of the blackout with us.

Special thanks are due to Wayne Barrett, a journalist and an associate at the Columbia University Graduate School of Journalism, who did much of the work leading to the analysis in Chapters VII and VIII, and to Susan Schraga, a research associate at the New York City Victims Service Agency. Thanks also to Prof. James Levine of the Political Science Department of Brooklyn College and Prof. Penn Kimball of the Columbia University Graduate School of Journalism whose suggestions were extremely helpful.

The field work was greatly aided by several research assistants, among them, Nancy Hornstein, a student at Hofstra Law School; Douglas Williams, a political science student at Brooklyn College; and Joel Bennett, a student at the Columbia University Graduate School of Journalism. Typing of the early drafts was done by Ann Gravitch and, of the final report, by Les Von Losberg.

While we relied on the help of many people and agencies, the findings and interpretations in this book are solely the responsibility of the two authors.

THE PURPOSE OF THIS STUDY

By all estimates, in both financial and social terms the blackout looting was very costly to New York, which was already shaken by its fiscal crisis. City officials estimated that the blackout would cost businesses $135 million to $150 million in theft and other property damage out of a total bill in the hundreds of millions of dollars, including a lost work day for most New Yorkers. This estimate did not take into account sales losses for businesses that closed the day after the blackout. The city's Office of Economic Development put property losses of 1,576 businesses at $38,290,100. The city government's own costs were estimated at $12 million to $15 million, much of it in overtime pay. Con Edison estimated a $5.5 million loss in revenues.

It was suspected that the widespread looting would further frighten inhabitants of neighborhoods adjacent to the looted areas where residents and business people were on the fence about remaining in the city. According to Victor Marrero, former chairman of the New York City Planning Commission, the city has invested a great deal of time and money in efforts to stabilize such neighborhoods, and much of it may be lost.

It is difficult to assess the personal losses to individual merchants, citizens who were injured, and police and firemen who risked their own safety. For many, the whole affair was no less than a devastating tragedy. Equally significant but more difficult to calculate was the damage to black-white relations. Although looters were generally unconcerned with race, white merchants were overwhelmingly their victims. In the aftermath it was apparent that the blackout had rekindled strong racial antagonisms.

* * *

While this study will analyze the results of the blackout looting in some detail, it is primarily concerned with the causes—with answering questions having to do with "why." Why, for instance, was there no similar outbreak the last time the lights went out, in 1965? On that night, New Yorkers of all classes and in all neighborhoods reacted with a cool that became part of the city's folklore. Not only did people feel a sudden surge of community spirit, but also had a remarkably diminished urge to commit crimes. Only a handful of stores were looted that night, and crime in general dipped precipitously. Indeed such exemplary behavior in 1965 might largely explain the sense of shock, hurt and anger with which most New Yorkers greeted the massive looting in 1977. It also gives urgency to the question of how two seemingly similar incidents could produce such radically different reactions.

Fairly simple to pinpoint are the merely accidental but nevertheless profound differences between the two nights. In 1965 it was a cool November evening, with temperatures ranging from 43 to 48 degrees; people in poor neighborhoods were not out on the streets in great numbers. The sky was also clear, with a full moon which cast at least some light down on the city. More significant was the different timing of the two blackouts. When the lights went out at 5:30 P.M. in 1965, store owners were still in their shops, locking up for the night. Many decided to stay on through the evening, which deterred any looting. On July 13, 1977, the city went dark at 9:35 P.M., when the only shops generally open were liquor stores, small groceries, and here and there a drug store. All others had closed for the night. Considering the subsequent tendency of the looters to shun stores that were occupied, it seems reasonable to assume that the looting would have been much less widespread had the lights gone out a little earlier in the evening.

Also important is the fact that 1965 marked the city's first large-scale blackout, and no one was certain that power would be lost for an extended period of time. In 1977 New Yorkers had already participated in a blackout, and most were convinced immediately that the city was in for a long spell with no electricity, no appliances, and no water for some tenants in high rises.

Questions having to do with underlying causes, however, raise considerably more problems. Not in recent memory, in fact, has a local issue caused such widespread concern and such heated argument. One interesting aspect of the debate, aired most prominently on the Op Ed Page and in the letters columns of the *New York Times*, was how fully social attitudes seem to have changed since the late 1960s. Attempts to explain the looting as emanating from the same sources of frustration that had driven the urban rioters of ten years before lost much of their power to convince. Conservatives were condemnatory, of course, but so were many people who regard themselves as social liberals. A *New York Times*/CBS poll of attitudes found that 60 percent of New Yorkers thought the looters "are the kind of people who always steal. . . ." Because it emphasized personal gain rather than politics, the looting struck many people as ideologically empty: a temporary escape from poverty rather than a lashing out at perceived oppression. Those who maintained that the looter, like the rioter, might be "saying" something, as one writer argued, failed to see the difference "between a hoodlum and a dissident."

Since the looting, we have visited almost every community in the city where looting occurred, and some where it did not. We have interviewed more than two hundred people, including city officials, policemen, merchants, looters, community leaders and local residents. In addition we have read and analyzed official reports from the Planning Department, the Police Department, the New York City Criminal Justice Agency, the New York State Criminal Justice Division, the city's Economic Development Agency and others.

We will present the facts as best we can as to the nature, extent and style of the looting. We shall also discuss who participated, who was arrested and how the police responded. We will then try to decode any messages that were transmitted that night to see what they can tell us about the conditions of the urban poor, and whether ghetto neighborhoods have changed since the rioting drew our attention there a decade ago.

BLACKOUT LOOTING!

THE THREE STAGES OF LOOTING

By all accounts the looting broke out spontaneously and generally in all five boroughs between ten minutes and half an hour after the lights went out at about 9:35 P.M.[1] At police headquarters in Manhattan, the first word that people were breaking into stores did not arrive until 10:00 P.M. But on Utica Avenue in Crown Heights, some reported that the lights had hardly dimmed before the looting began. Brother Ramzas, for instance, a community leader and the owner of Muslim Jewelry on Utica Avenue, said he arrived at his store at 9:45 P.M. to find his gates ripped off and looters pouring out of the door, carrying all his merchandise. In Bedford-Stuyvesant, the owner of Discount Liquors at Throop and Fulton Streets said the looting began five or ten minutes after the blackout. "It was almost like they came out of the air," he said. In the Bronx, police commanders and community people put the starting time at fifteen to twenty minutes after darkness descended; this was just time enough, said Captain Gallagher of the 44th Precinct, "for people to realize the lights weren't going to come back on."

In Bushwick, Aubrey Edmonds, a coordinator for the Bushwick Youth Services, said it was immediately after the blackout that crowds formed, waiting for the first spark. When the lights went out Edmonds was walking back from Broadway on Schaefer Street, and he noticed small knots of people gathering. "There were groups standing on the corners, mumbling and talking to themselves," Edmonds said. "They were trying to get up the energy to do something. They knew something had to be done that night; it was just a question of when someone was going to get it started." He thinks it was twenty minutes before someone got a car and drove through the iron gates of a sporting goods store on Broadway at Decatur Street. At that point a crowd swarmed in, assaulted the white owner and cleaned out the merchandise. Shortly thereafter, the store was set afire.

The astonishing spontaneity of the looting is more understandable when we examine the process of events and analyze the different groups of people who participated once the looting was underway. In their studies of the numerous riots in the 1960s, Quarantelli and Dynes have discovered that looting occurred following the initiation of civil disturbances.[2] The disturbances as a whole, they found, generally progressed in three stages.

In the first stage, destruction rather than plunder appears to be the rioters' intent. It is often initiated by alienated adolescents or ideologically motivated agitators in a specific area.

In the second stage, there is conscious and deliberate looting, and the taking of goods is organized and systematic. This stage is often dominated by delinquent gangs and theft groups operating with pragmatic rather than ideological considerations.

In the third stage there is an open, widespread and nonsystematic taking of goods. At this point, plundering becomes the normative, the socially supported thing to do; people from all social and income levels who reside in the community participate. Thus first there are rioters; then there are looters.[3]

While our judgments about who was involved in the looting—and when—are influenced by the Quarantelli-Dynes formulation, the stages of looting participation differ in an important way from those in the 1960s rioting.

Our evidence shows that through the night and into the morning, the looting drew in some proportion of people from all strata that live in poor communities. But judging from eyewitness reports and from analyses of data provided by the New York City Criminal Justice Agency and the New York City Police Department on those arrested, the make-up of the looters changed during the course of the blackout. While, obviously, no precise cut-off time can be established for a shift from one type of participant to another, the looting appeared to be divided into three stages that drew in three types of people.

From the time the lights went out until about 10:30 or 11:00 P.M., the looting was overwhelmingly performed by criminal types who opened the stores and swept in quickly to take away the most valuable merchandise. These looters were mainly men between the ages of twenty and thirty. In normal times they virtually command the streets and live by various sorts of dealing, theft and hustling. They need no blackout to engage in crime. Indeed, Table I-1 shows that 81.5 percent of those arrested in the first hour of the blackout had previous arrest records. This early participant we label the Stage I looter.

It is important to note that in this first stage there was virtually no law enforcement. Initiators of the looting, the street types, were in control of events, even to the extent, as we will detail later, of keeping other potential looters out of stores until they had cleaned out the best merchandise for themselves.

In the Stage II period, the looters were joined by bands of youths, alienated adolescents who were looking for fun and excitement, but who also seized the opportunity to gain free material goods and money in the chaos they helped to create. As Table I-2 indicates, once involved, youths sixteen to

Table I-1

FIRST ARREST BY TIME OF ARREST

	2130–2230 July 13, 1977		0001–0300 July 14, 1977		1100–1400 July 14, 1977	
First Arrest	5	(18.5%)	36	(33.0%)	13	(44.8%)
Not First Arrest	22	(81.5%)	73	(67.0%)	16	(55.2%)
Total	27	(100.0%)	109	(100.0%)	29	(100.0%)
Missing Values	4		9		0	

Source: NYC Criminal Justice Agency, January 1978

twenty years old participated quite extensively throughout the entire blackout.

While they made up only 15 percent of the first hour arrestees, they comprised more than 40 percent of both subsequent groups later arrested. Also entering the looting in the Stage II period were the generally unemployed, badly educated, ghetto poor under thirty-five years of age, who saw no reason not to join in the stealing.

The third stage, which generally began between 11:00 P.M.

Table I-2

AGE BY TIME OF ARREST

	2130–2230 July 13, 1977		0001–0300 July 14, 1977		1100–1400 July 14, 1977	
16–20	4	(14.8%)	45	(43.3%)	11	(45.8%)
21–25	8	(29.6%)	25	(24%)	9	(37.5%)
26–30	6	(22.2%)	17	(16.3%)	2	(8.3%)
31–40	7	(25.9%)	12	(11.5%)	1	(4.2%)
41+	2	(7.4%)	5	(4.8%)	1	(4.2%)
Total	27	(99.9%)	104	(99.9%)	24	(100.0%)
Missing Values	4		14		5	

Source: NYC Criminal Justice Agency, January 1978

and midnight, and stretched into the next afternoon, involved the stable poor and working-class members of the community who were caught up by the near hysteria in the streets. Legal constraints against stealing had suddenly been lifted. Social pressure to "dip in" and take something was far greater than the normal pressure to abide by the law. The force loose in the street also drew in a second type of Stage III looter: the better off, employed, neighborhood resident who seemed to be motivated by abject greed. Unlike the Stage I looter, the Stage III person had little or no experience in crime, and was likely to have family and community ties. Stage III looters were encouraged by the early blackout situation, during which they perceived no risk of arrest. Unfortunately for them, however, the Stage III looters appeared in large numbers at the same time the police were reaching sufficient strength to begin regaining control of the streets.

To test the stage theory we took profiles of three groups of arrestees by time of arrest. The first group is a universe of those who were picked up between 9:35 and 10:35 P.M. in certain precincts that kept sufficient data on time of arrest. The second group is a sample of people arrested from midnight to 3:00 A.M. The third group is a sample of alleged looters arrested between 11:00 A.M. and 2:00 P.M. on July 14,[4] Table I shows that nearly 82 percent of those arrested during the first hour of the blackout had been arrested before; this clearly indicates a high degree of prior criminal activity. The number of those with previous arrests drops to 67 percent for the second group arrested from midnight to 3:00 A.M., and declines further, to 55 percent, for the third group, which was arrested during the middle of the day. While a 55 percent prior arrest rate may seem high to middle-class readers, it is important to note that in 1968 the President's Commission on the Study of Crime and Delinquency found that anywhere from 50 to 90 percent of black urban males have arrest records.[5]

The data in Table II further support the notion of a significant change in the looting population as the disorder progressed. Only 15 percent of the first-hour arrestees were in the sixteen-to-twenty age group. By midnight the number had climbed to 43 percent, and it remained at that level in the mid-day group.

The Stage I looter could perhaps best be typified by Willis Barnes, a sharp-witted, chunky, thirty-one-year-old black man born and raised in Brooklyn, who works as a furniture mover and as a professional criminal. His second profession, it seems, has occupied more of his time, considering that he has spent ten of the last thirteen years in jail. The first arrest was for shooting an acquaintance to death shortly before graduating from Boys High School. Barnes claimed the other boy came at him with a knife. The district attorney said it was murder. They compromised, calling it manslaughter, and Willis did a six-year stretch. After that, he had two more jail terms, one for armed robbery, and one for "larceny by trick." He has spent time in nearly every prison in upstate New York, and has accumulated a year-and-a-half's worth of college credits toward a degree in computer science. He doesn't think he'll complete the degree, though, because of all the "other stuff" the degree would require.

Willis, who was interviewed as he sat talking with a girl-friend on a packing crate underneath the elevated subway on Broadway in Bushwick, was driving along Eastern Parkway the night the lights went out. He saw the looting start on Utica Avenue. "There was a lot of fear mixed with excitement," he said. "A lot of people didn't know what was going on, but when they saw all the looting, they got it on too. You see other people jump into a store and you said, 'I'm going too. I'm going in there and getting me something too.' "

"Right," chimed in his girlfriend, who was out on Broadway that night and remembers getting a $150 Panasonic radio which she sold for $100. "I got mine just like everyone got theirs."

"You could see," continued Willis, "that cops would chase people and fire a few shots in the air. But it didn't seem like they wanted to kill anyone. They just turned on their sirens and hoped that the people would run away. At first people were nervous, but after they got used to the dark and saw their families were together, it turned out to be a joke.''

For his part, Willis parked his car, gathered a couple of friends, and returned to Utica Avenue with a thirty-eight foot moving van to join the looting in a businesslike fashion. "You had young kids out there running all over, and anything they could grab, they grabbed," he said, somewhat contemptuously. "But then you had some high-class dudes. They left the wine alone and went to the Scotch and bourbon. This is the ghetto, and you got a lot of thieves here who know what to steal and what to leave alone. It all depends on the store, but they know what goes for money and that's what they steal.''

In a grocery, for instance, Willis would go for cans of salmon and tuna, pampers, and baby food. "You steal a color TV and I have a van loaded with pampers, and I bet I can sell all those pampers before you sell that TV. In the ghetto, people ain't got no money for color TVs, but they got a lot of babies, and they got to have pampers. Color TVs go well in working-class sections, where maybe people have only small bank accounts, but they got money coming every Tuesday or whatever, so you know you'll get paid.''

That night Willis and his two friends filled the truck twice with merchandise obtained from their looting forays all over Central Brooklyn. Among the goods they stole were forty-eight color TVs, three-piece suits, leather coats, suede coats, and sneakers.

Willis said he hadn't looted the stores as much as he had looted the looters. "What you'd do," he said, "is you park down the street from the store a little, and everyone's confused and running around. So you tell a guy, 'Hey, I got a truck for all this stuff,' and you tell him when he comes out to put it in there. After they've put a lot of stuff in, you just shut the door and drive off while they're in the store getting more."

Willis thinks the looters were just acting naturally—that any normal person would steal if he were convinced he would never be punished. "Everyone's got a little thievery, a little wrong in them," he said. "It's nature. You're walking down the street and there's a store open, and there's TVs and stuff in there, and won't nothing happen to you if you go in and get it. You wouldn't go in and get one?"

* * *

deter. of Stage II looters

The Stage II looter was typified by young, unattached men, poorly educated and only sporadically employed, who have a long record of failure at every endeavor middle-class culture deems valuable, and a growing involvement in street hustling and criminal activity. This is a fairly accurate picture of Jeff Freeman, a twenty-year-old, tall, muscular, restless young man who lives in the Bronx and was active in looting in the Concourse area.

Jeff never knew his father, and his mother died from alcoholism when he was small. He grew up in various households comprised of his aunts, sisters, and other extended family members. He got as far as his junior year in high school when he had a fight with a teacher who tried to "mess" with him. The teacher, according to Jeff, suffered a broken leg in the confrontation, and Jeff was expelled. After that he went into a Texas Job Corps camp which turned into another disaster. While working on the roof of a construction project, Jeff accidentally cut off his right thumb with a circular saw. The boy in back of him started laughing. Furious, Jeff hit him on the head with a board, which led to Jeff's expulsion from the Job Corps. A subsequent lawsuit over his lost thumb won Jeff $5,000, but this was paid out in monthly installments and is long since gone.

Jeff cannot read so much as a menu. Since leaving high school five years ago, he has held only one job for any length of time, and that for just three weeks as a watchman at a furniture store. It paid $100 a week, but Jeff quit because the boss "tried to order me around." Anyway, work that pays only $100 a week he ridicules contemptuously as a mere "job job." He says he needs much more than that to live.

Despite his illiteracy and his total unsalability in the job market, Jeff has fairly conventional aims for his life. Most important, because he never had a home, he wants his own place, a studio apartment. "I don't want to sleep on nobody's couch or nobody's floor or hallway," he says. He also wants to "travel." And when asked what kind of job he would eventually want, he said that someday he would like to join the Army. Considering his illiteracy and lack of a high school diploma, this is not a likely possibility.

While Jeff is not, and perhaps never will be, as smooth and sharp as Willis Barnes, the only thing at which he is remotely successful is small-time street hustling and, we suspect, pimping. He still talks continuously of how tough he is and just what he would do if anyone messed with him. (What he would do, he demonstrated, is to take a small penknife he carries in his shirt and quickly stick the point into the vicinity of the attacker's carotid artery. "A little knife is good enough, if you know how to use it," he said.) "I don't care about anything," he stated, in describing his street life. "If I can see where I can get it and not go nowhere [to jail], then I'm gonna get it. My only friend is a dollar bill," he added, in what seems to be an oft-repeated maxim. When asked where he might like to travel someday, he said he'd like to go to North Vietnam where the "Cong" are. Obviously, this is a trip which would enhance his image on the street. Jeff has never heard of the NAACP, the Urban League or Andrew Young.

While he has few conventional skills, Jeff did demonstrate considerable ingenuity during the looting. He was on University Avenue when the lights went out, but waited until 11:00 P.M. before risking involvement in the looting himself. "I always think before I move," he said. "I didn't want to be in some store when boom! the lights go on." When he thought it ~~Co. tires~~ was safe, he went up to an A&P supermarket and helped to pry open the gates with a crowbar. Then he wired four shopping carts together, loaded them with everything from canned goods to frozen turkeys, conveyed them three blocks to a girlfriend's house and wrestled them all up three flights of stairs. "The next day," he said, "I'll tell you, my arms was sore."

After that, he got a TV set and a stereo with a tape deck,

but was jostled by the crowd as he came out of the store, and dropped the television on the sidewalk. He said he gave up looting after that. The possessions he has from that night are the stereo and three looted presents given him by another girl-friend: a pair of $25-dark glasses, a $24-pendant, and a large brass ring formed in the head of an Indian chief that would have sold for $1.98.

* * *

The Stage III looter, represented by several different types of more stable community residents, both men and women, was not likely to be an initiator that night. After being assured there was little risk involved, the Stage III looter allowed him-self to be swept up by the feeling in the street and submitted to the strong social pressure to join in the stealing.

One kind of Stage III looter was Cindy Robinson, an eigh-teen-year-old unwed mother with a fourteen-month-old son. Cindy lives with her mother; both are unemployed and on welfare. Also in the household is Cindy's sister, who is twenty and has two children under the age of three. They are also on welfare. Cindy was home in her rather small, high-rise tenement apartment in Harlem when the lights went out. Her first reaction, she said, was to "go grab the babies."

Cindy did not go outside right away. In fact, she was so frightened that she went to bed and tried to sleep. Next door, however, a fire broke out and her mother made her get out of bed, fearful that the fire might spread to their apartment. Cindy looked out the window: "It was too dark; it was black; you couldn't see nothin' but people with flashlights and light-in' matches and everything, and then a bunch of boys was breaking in stores next door, on the corner, and they was get-tin' all kinds of food and everything, and me and my sister went down there and got some things."

When asked, why did you do it? she replied, ". . . every-body was doing it and it was free. I was right next door." Af-ter a pause she smiled and said, "I did it for the fun of it." Later in the interview, however, Cindy said that when she got into the store she looked for "baby food and pampers. I tried to find pampers but they beat me to 'em."

She didn't worry about being arrested since "everybody was doin' it, little kids and everything." When she returned to her apartment with her sister, they had acquired detergent, baby food, and a case of spinach.

Cindy did not know New York City had experienced a blackout in 1965; therefore she was unaware of the comparisons made in the press of the two events. But when informed of the 1965 blackout and the fact that there was almost no looting at that time, she said:

I think maybe they didn't loot too much before because the crisis wasn't too bad. But now you know everybody is down and everything without jobs. That's probably why it was more looters. . . . Maybe people had jobs then and . . . they didn't do too bad; the city wasn't low of money but now it's like that. Everybody's out of a job almost and you know everybody's down for stealing, and that's probably why there was more lootin'.

Some looters in Stage III were just as larcenous at heart as those in Stage I, but they delayed their participation for fear of losing whatever they had gained from their jobs.

Henry Simpson, a salesman in a downtown Brooklyn clothing store, was just coming out of the movie *Black Sunday* at Church and Rugby Avenues with his wife of eight years, when the lights went out. "When we reached the corner for the bus," he said, "I saw the deal. The lights were out as far as I could see in all directions. I got on the bus and I realized what was going on. I knew the power was off all over and that something was going to happen."

Born in Bedford-Stuyvesant, Henry was raised by his mother, a clerical worker, and received regular visits from his divorced father, who worked as a jewelry polisher in Manhattan. He graduated from high school and spent eighteen months in Vietnam as a paratrooper. In one incident near Pleiku, he was blown several feet in the air when an American .105 Howitzer shell landed short, killing two of his friends nearby. He came back to Brooklyn in 1969 and got a job selling clothes in a store in Manhattan. Five years later, he had an opportunity to make more money working in a bigger national chain clothing store in downtown Brooklyn. At the time of the looting he grossed about $225 a week. His paycheck, together with the $150 his wife earns as a billing clerk, gives his family $375 a week. This income is substantial enough for them to have an apartment along a good section of Bushwick Avenue, where they have lived for five years, and to send their nine-year-old son to parochial school, which costs $500 a year. As with other lower-middle class families, however, even though their total income seems fairly impressive when compared to the poverty index, it is heavily committed to payments for material things.

Henry said he likes to look back on each year and see what his money has done for him and his family. "At the end of every fiscal year I should have accomplished something. I don't want to work a whole year and have nothing to show for it. I see too many guys in a situation where they work year after year, and they got nothing to show." In 1975 Henry and his wife bought a lot of furniture for their apartment. In 1976 they spent a week in Bermuda.

In 1977 they bought a $9,300 Buick Electra 225 with all the trimmings: climate control, automatic doorlocks, tilting steering wheel, sunroof, eight-track stereo, and automatic trunk release. Henry put down $5,000 in cash, and he owes $150 a month for three years.

The night of the blackout, as he was taking his wife home on the bus, he saw looting going on and resolved to come back and get something he'd long wanted: a really good racing bicycle, the kind that costs $500 or $600. Even though bike riding is Henry's only hobby—he rides in Prospect Park, and is planning a trip to Bear Mountain—he said he never could have afforded $600 for a good bike. Henry knew of two bike shops, both on Flatbush Avenue, and thought he could get away with the theft. "The opportunity was there," he said several times. "I realized that if I wanted to take a shot at it, I could get away with it scot free. I could get it, and nothing would happen."

He said his wife argued and pleaded with him to stay home

that night. He told her "not to worry," got on his own bicycle, and rode back to Flatbush Avenue, where he arrived at about 10:30. Unfortunately for Simpson, the two bike shops were guarded, one by the owner and the other by the owner and a large dog. "It was now eleven o'clock and I felt it was too late to go to Nostrand and Fulton where I knew another bike shop was, so I gave up the idea." (That, too, would have netted him nothing since it was cleaned out early in the evening.)

The street meanwhile was becoming chaotic. "People were running around like crazy, like a pack of wild dogs," he said. "They started massing together to yank down the gates. All up and down Flatbush Avenue police cars were zooming up and down, but they had no effect. Just going up and down and up and down. There were too few of them and too many people. People were taking TVs, washing machines; the stuff too heavy to carry they just abandoned in the street."

Simpson said the urge to loot came over him in the midst of the chaos. "I don't know; I felt I wanted to snatch something while I was out there. I wasn't thinking about a color TV or anything that the professional dudes were after, like cars and things. I just wanted to snatch something."

It all happened too quickly, he said, to recall in detail. "I happened to be on the scene when they just began to break into this store," he said. "Things started flying out, and I happened to get my hands full of the stuff. And I was standing on the corner talking, when suddenly a police car pulls up, and they got me."

The officers took him down to the precinct and booked him for possession of stolen goods, which turned out to be ten pairs of women's slacks and seven blouses.

Looking back three weeks after his arrest, Simpson was not sure what he was doing with the women's clothes. They weren't for his wife, he said. He thinks maybe he was going to try to fence them. Whatever the reason, he sorely regrets the evening. After spending eight sweltering days locked in the Brooklyn House of Detention and various other places, Simpson returned to his job with the phony story that he was just an innocent bystander that night, and that it was all a big mistake. His boss, he said, agreed to give him the benefit of the doubt, but only if he could get his case dismissed. Simpson's Legal Aid lawyer (he also lied that he had no money so he could get a free lawyer) advised him that at best he may get a suspended sentence, which Simpson doesn't think will satisfy his employer.

"I can't return to the street without a job," he said. "I can't live off unemployment. That's what keeps me tossing and turning at night. I can't lose my job. I don't know what I'll do."*

Henry looks at his actions that night as wrong only because they got him in trouble. "There's a wallet on the floor and some money sticking out of it, and nobody's going to see you take it. That's what it was like, the same situation. I saw an opportunity and took advantage of it." He makes a distinction between that and actually initiating the looting or, for that matter, launching any criminal act. "I would never, like, do any stickups or mug someone," he said. "I would never have organized no group and go out and pry open the gates."

Simpson said he found it hard to explain these differences to his wife. "My wife got mad at me, as if I'd stolen something from her!" 'Why did you do it?' she says. But I was surprised she was surprised at my action. I just took a chance. I don't know anyone who's really gotten anywhere and didn't take a chance. Rockefeller and the Gettys—you know what their fathers were all about? Their fathers were murderers and thieves. They took a chance. They just got over."

The Shifting Stages

Comparing the Dynes and Quarantelli (D & Q) stages of participation in the 1960s rioting with those of the 1977 loot-

---

*A year and a half after the blackout, Henry's case was finally adjudicated. He agreed to plead guilty to a charge of possession of stolen goods and was fined $100. He also kept his job.

ing, one can find significant differences. In general the D & Q first stage—in which the desire to destroy stores predominated over the desire to steal goods—was nearly absent on the night of the blackout. This is not to say that there was no destruction or, in particular, heavy arson during the looting. But as we will detail later on, the penchant to burn and destroy was not universal in the city. Arson was largely confined to special areas, such as Broadway in Bushwick, and should not be used to describe the general behavior of looters at any time during the night. Where destruction occurred, it was usually a concomitant of stealing: that is, plate glass windows were smashed, shelves ripped off walls or spilled over in aisles, and doors wrenched off hinges.

Thus the 1977 looting seems to have begun at the D & Q second-stage level, with systematic and methodical stealing. As for the D & Q third stage—the general involvement of all classes—in our analysis, we have broken it into two stages (Stage II and Stage III), largely because of more detailed police arrest data.

An important question, however, still remains: how does one explain the shift in participation in the course of the blackout, particularly the shift that brought in the more stable elements of the community in Stage III? Dynes and Quarantelli say that underlying the shift from limited underclass participation to widespread involvement of large numbers of people representative of all segments of the ghetto community is a temporary and localized redefinition of property rights. In situations of this kind, they agree, "rights to the use of existing resources become problematical, and in many instances there are open challenges to prior ownership. And if property is thought of as the shared understanding of who can do what with the value resources within a community, in civil disorders there occurs a breakdown in this understanding."[6] What was previously taken for granted, they suggest, now becomes a matter of open dispute, and is expressed concretely in a redefinition of existing property rights.

Indeed, looters in the 1977 blackout often seemed unconcerned about the picture they presented to outsiders of themselves as thieves. And the involvement of so many people, many of whom would never under normal circumstances commit a crime, raises deeper questions about what is really happening in the minds of people who seem to lose all concern for law. In this regard, Dynes and Quarantelli offer an important insight into the underlying dynamics of this kind of behavior. But their notion seems to be based on an assumption that property rights and their relationship to other values are similarly held throughout the entire population. There is reason to believe they are not.

For many reasons, and because of a variety of social and economic forces, large numbers of ghetto residents live as Tally did in *Tally's Corner*, Elliot Liebow's classic study of the rootless, black male denizen of a Washington, D.C., street corner. Tally is representative of a lower-class life style that holds what Liebow calls a shadow system of values. That is to say, members of the lower class "share the general values of the society with members of other classes, but in addition they have stretched these values, or developed alternative ones which help them adjust to their deprived circumstances."[7]

For example, Tally accepts the value of marriage and family. But because his world, his lack of education and style of life deny him success in the workplace and at home, his experience with marriage amounts to a series of transitory relationships. After each episode he returns to the streetcorner where a shadow system of values deems his failure with women acceptable and permits him to be a man once again.[8]

Thus members of the lower class maintain a belief in the same values as everyone else. Their values, however, are not held in the same hierarchy as the parent or general system of values. Some values that are highly important to the larger society may be "subsidiary in nature, thinner and less weighty, less completely internalized."[9] The possibility that those who hold these values could shift to an entirely different system of behavior, does not lie far beneath the surface.

Moreover there has been a significant decline in legitimacy in society, and it cuts across all classes and racial groups. Values have changed. One can read almost as much about white-collar crime in government and business as about crime in the streets. If a shadow hierarchy of values is shaped by economic and cultural circumstances, it is likely also to be influenced by widespread criminal behavior in the entire society. Often, looters told us, they acted as anyone would. This is their exaggerated justification, of course, but to some extent they make a point.

ii

WHAT WAS LOOTED

Ted Gurr, in *Why Men Rebel*, tells us that there are several types of collective disturbances which occur at a surprisingly high frequency around the world.[1] The first and most common is a political disturbance in which violence is aimed at a regime or another group of people. A variety of grievances may underlie the conflict, and the violence is directed at resolving those grievances and gaining power and position to improve the status of those who seek change.

A second type of upheaval is a "welfare" disturbance, in which the objectives are economic or material. The violence is aimed at getting goods, more money, and more housing. However, the means of acquiring these things do not involve gaining a different or more favorable political position.

It seems clear that the blackout looting was basically a welfare disturbance, and only secondarily a political one. The prevailing tone of the looters was nonpolitical, and their purpose was to acquire items to fulfill personal needs or to sell to make money. That it was a welfare disturbance, however, does not suggest that the poor have lost their interest in political issues. It is just that the priority in this instance was obviously direct material gain.

As such, the looting was fairly selective and limited to the large stores located along commercial spines that sold food, clothing or easily-fenced goods. The Spanish bodegas, which were open at the time, and small shops and ghetto businesses along the side streets in the neighborhoods themselves, were generally passed over. While the image of the looting created in the press was that it was aimed at acquiring TVs, transistor radios, jewelry and other fenceable goods, it is important to note that the two most often struck stores—accounting for more than a third of the total—were those that sold food and clothing. Of the 1,328* looted stores surveyed by the Planning Commission, 288 of them sold wearing apparel, and 179 were food markets.

The other major categories were as follows:

Furniture and home furnishings	119
Household appliances	117
Variety	72
Jewelry	67
Drugstores	59
Restaurants/diners	55
Liquor	51
Automotive	49
Hardware	25
Sporting goods	25
Cleaners	17
Pawnshops	10

Some of the looted stores deserve a brief comment. The drugstores did not seem to be looted for the purpose of getting

*This figure, as will shortly be noted, does not include 288 additional stores added to the list from a separate count by the Police Department.

drugs, but rather for the extensive line of merchandise most of them now carry. Liquor stores rate only ninth on the list because, as noted in the introduction, they tended to be open and doing business at the time of the blackout. What is more, liquor store proprietors, compared with their fellow shop owners, seem to be fairly well armed.

Automotive stores were hard hit, it was pointed out, because poor people frequently don't use garages when their cars break down; rather, they buy parts and fix the cars themselves.

In one of the few expeditions into white areas, thirty minutes after the blackout men in a truck pulled up in front of the Zermo Gun Co. on Warren Street in the otherwise quiet Wall Street area, pulled off its steel grating, and neatly made off with an indeterminate number of guns.

Easily the biggest score of the evening came at the Ace Pontiac Co. in the middle of the used-car district on Jerome Avenue in the Bronx. According to the owner, who was informed by witnesses, between 10:00 and 11:00 P.M. some 200 people came crashing through his plate-glass windows and headed for the 55 brand-new cars stored in the back garage. Each, in accordance with fire laws, had two dollars' worth of gas in the tank and the keys dangling from the ignition. Then, in an incredible feat of organizational skill, they managed to drive fifty of the cars out a single door and off into the night. "They love Pontiacs, that's all," said the owner, when asked why no other car place was hit. "They love Pontiacs, they just love them." Of the fifty cars stolen, forty-nine were eventually recovered. Some of them, obviously driven by people who didn't know how to drive, were found smashed into light poles a block from the garage. Others had just run out of the $2.00 worth of gas. And twenty-two of the forty-nine recovered were stripped down to the chassis. Windshields had been taken out, and steering wheels, transmissions, dashboards were neatly disassembled. Asked whether he thought the stripping was organized by professionals, the owner replied: "They're *all* professionals out there! There are thousands of them!"

While they have no place on the store list, the most frequently looted items that night were sneakers. Thousands and
thousands of pairs found feet before sunrise. In sporting
goods stores, they were the first to go. They drew looters to
shoe stores. They caused many break-ins in clothing stores.
On Amsterdam Avenue at 92nd Street an owner of a TV store
claims the looters were so busy at a sneaker store down the
block that they left him alone. "If you had sneakers [in your
store] that night," said Captain Clifford of the 41st Precinct in
the South Bronx, "you were in big trouble." On this scale,
the person in the worst trouble of all was the owner of "The
Sneaker King" on Willis Avenue in the South Bronx. His
shop consists of a string of four stores linked together, all
filled, floor to ceiling, with sneakers. In a brief orgy of sneaker acquisition that night, the looters quickly cleaned him out.

Extent of the Looting

In all, 1,616* stores suffered damage during the blackout.
While in only one instance—on Broadway in Brooklyn—did
the looting reach the peak of destruction that characterized
the 1960s rioting, no poor area in any of the five boroughs was
left untouched. At least thirty-one separate neighborhoods
experienced considerable destruction or stealing. Groups of
black and white teenagers roamed the streets, breaking windows on Bay Street in the Stapleton section of Staten Island,
a neighborhood which looks only slightly disheveled compared to the city's better-known slums. Looting went on in
Lefrak City, a racially mixed middle-class section of Rego
Park, Queens, where people smashed the front door of a Path-
mark Drug Store and made off with several cartons of ciga-
rettes. To the north, two stores in the Co-op City complex in

---

*This is the total collated by the Planning Commission from its own survey and
that of the police.

the Bronx were struck, even though the lights there had not gone out. To the south, thirty-four stores were reported looted or damaged in the Coney Island section of Brooklyn along Mermaid and Surf Avenues.

Damage varied significantly from section to section, as did the extent of the stealing. Stores in Queens and Staten Island typically had only a window broken and perhaps their display cases cleaned out. On Broadway in Bushwick, a Woolworth's was not only sacked, but was then put to the torch and burned so thoroughly that the following week nothing remained but for a bulldozer to level it to the ground.

Looting in the Bronx and Brooklyn was by far the most destructive.[2] Of the 473 stores damaged in the Bronx, 78 (or 16 percent) were also burned. In Brooklyn, 119 (also 16 percent) of the 705 affected stores were set afire, whereas in Manhattan, only 17 of the 348 stores reported fire damage. Fire Chief Miley of the 12th Battalion in East Harlem said that "other nights on weekends have been just as bad or worse." Little fire damage was reported in Queens where 80 stores were looted; no fires occurred on Staten Island, where 10 stores reported damage. Similarly Bronx and Brooklyn looters tended to deal with the stores more harshly. In the two respective boroughs, 48 percent and 44 percent of the stores reported "major" interior damage, while only 26 percent of the Manhattan stores were hit that hard.

The difference in damage in the various boroughs was also reflected in store reopenings. The day after the blackout, a planning department survey found 68 percent of the Manhattan stores already reopened for business. This contrasted with only 47 percent for the Bronx and 36 percent for Brooklyn.

With the large amount of arson in certain areas that night, the fire department was just as overtaxed as the police. In what it considers the blackout period—from 9:30 P.M. on Wednesday to 9:00 A.M. on Friday, or about 36 hours—the NYFD received 3,900 alarms and fought 1,037 fires. Because the fires were more serious than normal, the department had to ignore 1,677 of the 3,900 alarms.[3] Just how many blazes burned unattended, it is impossible to say.

The 1,037 fires fought during that period was an increase of 25 percent over the 836 fires fought during a comparable period the week before, on July 7th, 8th and 9th. As previously noted, the blackout fires were much more intense than normal. There were 14 multiple-alarm fires, and one five-alarmer, that night compared to only 4 the week before. Some 47 of the blackout fires called for "all hands," which means using three engines, two ladder trucks and a battalion chief, as opposed to 26 during the same period the week before.

Of the borough totals, Brooklyn suffered 303 fires that night (7 multiple alarms, 20 "all hands"); the Bronx had 307 (3 multiple alarms, 14 "all hands"); Manhattan had 209 (1 multiple alarm, 3 "all hands"); Queens, 134 (2 multiple alarms, 3 "all hands"); and Staten Island, 45.

The most awesome damage by far occurred along a thirty-block stretch of Broadway in Brooklyn that serves as the dividing line between Bushwick to the north and Bedford-Stuyvesant to the south. Of the 134 stores looted in that section, 45, or 33 percent, were damaged by fire; many of these were burned to the ground. Commercial life here was certainly ailing before the blackout. But afterward, walking down what five years ago was a thriving business street, a shopper could go for blocks and find absolutely no merchandise for sale. For four blocks, from Gates to Linden to Quincy to Grove, every major store still doing business at the time of the blackout was looted clean, and a majority of them were also burned.

Overhead the elevated subway line closes out the sun, giving an added sense of desolation to the street. Hollowed-out storefronts stand bleakly along rubbish-strewn sidewalks, their iron gates wrenched apart as if by a giant hand. Only one supermarket was open a month after the blackout in a fifteen-block stretch. Except for rush hours, the avenue is nearly deserted. Here and there an elderly person sits on a kitchen chair staring into the street; children play in the debris; and unemployed men tinker over the engine of a rusted-out car. Sometimes the only sound comes from the basement of gutted buildings where water splashes out from broken pipes.

In contrast to the destruction along Broadway, other areas were looted more cleanly. The only signs a week and a half later that anything had happened were new steel gates, freshly glazed plate glass and an occasional sign advertising a "riot sale."

Another hard-hit section was a five-block strip of Utica Avenue in the Crown Heights section of Brooklyn, where seventy-five stores were cleaned out from Eastern Parkway to Montgomery Street. Along with its traditional mixture of stores, this section is also the headquarters for Caribbean jewelry craftsmen, twenty of whose shops were struck that night.

Table II-1 contains a list of the looted stores prepared by the Planning Department from its own survey and that taken by the Police Department. All the designations are self-explanatory except for the term "stem commercial," which stands for major cross streets where some looting also occurred close to the main commercial strip.

Table II-1
BRONX BLACKOUT AREAS

Commercial Strip	Strip Boundaries	Cross Streets	Stern Commercial	Number of Stores Affected
E. Tremont Ave.	401–1055 E. Tremont	E. Tremont from Webster to Boston Rd.	Boston Rd., off E. Tremont	58
Jerome Ave.	1771–2421 Jerome	E. 167th to E. Fordham Rd.	E. 174th off Jerome	25
E. 167th St.	86–374 E. 167th	Grand Concourse to Webster Ave.	Morris Ave. off 167th	44
Burnside Ave.	106–270 W. Burnside to E. Burnside	University Ave. to Webster		43
E. 170th St.	5–546 E. 170th	Jerome to Third Aves.	Clay Ave. off 3rd Ave.	32
E. 138th St.	472–581 E. 138th	Willis to Cypress Aves.	Park Ave. off 138th.	22
Grand Concourse	2159–2479 Grand Concourse	Burnside to Fordham		54
University Ave.	1712–1997 University	W. Tremont Ave. to Burnside	Featherbed Lane off University	21
Ogden Ave.	993–1282 Odgen	W. 164th to W. 170th	includes Gerard and Sedgwick Aves. off 170th	14
HUB	301–428 E. 149th.	Morris to Bergen	3rd Ave. off 149th E. 156th off	22
E. 183rd St.	101–223 E. 183rd	Morris to Grand Concourse	Westchester Ave.	12

Source: Department of City Planning

Southern Blvd.	942–1221 Southern	E. 163rd to E. 167 St.	Wilkins Ave.	9
Selected blocks on Prospect Ave., Southern Blvd.				24
E. 134th, 110th, 141 Sts. Jackson (isolated stores on these streets) in Prospect				
Mt. Eden Ave.	2–55 E. Mt. Eden	Jerome to Walton	includes Grand Concourse off Mt. Eden	10
West Tremont Ave.	102–158 W. Tremont	Featherbed Lane from University to Jerome		7
Southern Blvd.	E. 163 to Westchester	Aldus St.	Intervale, Longwood Ave., Prospect Ave.	7
Selected blocks on Bronxwood, Laconia Ave. E. Gun Hill Rd., White Plains Rd., in Williamsbridge				7
Fordham Road	19–696 E. Fordham	Morris to Southern Blvd	E. Tremont off Bronx River Parkway	12
Bathgate			Selected blocks on 3rd Ave. off 163rd, Webster off E. 169th, Bathgate off 172nd, Claremont off 3rd in Bathgate	12

BROOKLYN BLACKOUT AREAS

Commercial Strip	Strip Boundaries	Cross Streets	Stem Commercial	Number of Stores Affected
Broadway/Bushwick	773–2009 Broadway	Flushing to Eastern Pkwy	Stone Ave. off Bway. St. John's Place off East. Pkwy., Franklin Ave. nr. Atlantic Ave. & East. Pkwy	134
Utica Ave.	188–435 Utica	Atlantic Ave. to Empire Blvd.		104
5th Ave. in Sunset Park	4506–6016 5th; 13th Ave. & 38 & 78th Sts.	45th St. to 61st St.	7th Ave. & 15th St. 8th Ave. & 56th St.	56
Flatbush Ave.	616–1335 Flatbush	Parkside to Foster	18th Ave. & 86th St. Tilden, Church, Beverly Rds., Parkside Ave., New-kirk, Cortelyou Rds., Bedford—all off Flatbush	49
Myrtle Ave.	204–513 Myrtle	Flatbush to Washington Ave.	Ashland, Hanson Pl., So. Oxford off Fulton, Dekalb Ave. from Flatbush to Washington	28
Sutter Ave.	596–1205 Sutter	Pennsylvania to Euclid Aves.	Blake Ave., Van Siclen Sheffield, Shephard near Pennsylvania Ave.	22
Pitkin Ave.	1540–2768 Pitkin	East. Pkwy to Euclid Ave.		21

Location	Address Range	Boundaries		No.
Mermaid Ave.	1501–2327 Mermaid	Stillwell Ave. to W. 23rd St.	Kings Hwy. off Stillwell	34
Dekalb Ave.	495–905 Dekalb	Classon Ave. to Stuyvesant	Selected blocks on Myrtle, Gates, Nostrand, Ralph, Throop, Lewis, Franklin, Lafayette & March Aves., off Dekalb	49
Belmont Ave.	51–95 Belmont	Rockaway to Van Sinderen	Sutter Ave. & Saratoga Ave. off Rockaway	12
Nostrand Ave.	541–1915 Nostrand	Atlantic to Foster Aves.		45
Rutland Rd.	976–1104 Rutland	91st to 98th Sts.		19
Fulton St. (Bedford-Stuyvesant)	1165–1543 Fulton St.	Bedford to Albany		11
Rockaway Ave.	430–767 Rockaway	Eastern Pkwy. to Livonia Ave.		14
Broadway in Williamsburg near Flushing Ave.				22
Church Ave.	2287–5709 Church	Bedford to Kings Hwy.		17

BROOKLYN BLACKOUT AREAS

Commercial Strip	Strip Boundaries	Cross Streets	Stem Commercial	Number of Stores Affected
5th Ave.	153–538 5th	Flatbush to Prospect Ave.		14
Washington Ave. in Prospect Hgts.	759–857 Washington	Prospect Pl. to East. Pkwy.	Classon, Grand Vanderbilt near Washington	7
	354–449 Fulton St.	Adams St. to Flatbush	Willoughby off Fulton, Smith, Bridge Sts., Livingston St. off Flatbush	17
New Lots Ave.	213–777 New Lots	Van Sinderen to Shepard		8
Havemeyer St.	148–181 Havemeyer	S. 1st St. to S. 3rd St.	Roebling off 1st	7
Pennsylvania Ave.	249–1111 Pennsylvania	Pitkin to Flatlands Aves.	Livonia off Penna.	6

MANHATTAN BLACKOUT AREAS

Commercial Strip	Strip Boundaries	Cross Streets	Stem Commercial	Number of Stores Affected
Upper 3rd Ave.	1868–2289 Third	E. 102nd to E. 125th Sts.	116th & 125th Sts. off 2nd Ave.	75
St. Nicholas Ave. in Washington Heights	3815–4910 Broadway 1016–1654 St. Nicholas 2034–2088 Amsterdam Ave.	W. 159th & W. 172nd Sts. W. 167th to Fairview Ave. W. 161st to W. 164th Sts.	Audobon Ave. off 181st St.	40
Delancy Street/ Clinton Street			Orchard, Stanton, 31 Grand Sts.; from Essex to Orchard	
Broadway–West Side	1875–2833 Broadway	W. 62nd St. to Cathedral Pkway		39
Upper Broadway	2878–3627 Broadway	W. 111th to W. 151st Sts.		21
Lenox Ave.	139–613 Lenox	W. 116th to W. 141st Sts.	W. 125th St. off 8th Ave.	34
8th Ave.	2027–2803 8th	W. 116th to W. 151st Sts.		
Dyckman St.	118–213 Dyckman	Sherman Ave. to Bway.		14
W. 116th St. & W. 125th St.	68–610 W. 125th 68–254 W. 116th	Lenox to Riverside Dr. Lenox to 8th		21

MANHATTAN BLACKOUT AREAS

Commercial Strip	Strip Boundaries	Cross Streets	Stern Commercial	Number of Stores Affected
Amsterdam Ave.	520–948 Amsterdam	W. 86th to W. 107th Sts.	W. 104th off Amsterdam, W. 96th St. off Amsterdam	16
Broadway in Midtown	1147–1519 Broadway	W. 28th to W. 45th Sts.	36th St. off 7th Ave. 45th St. off 6th Ave. Lincoln Plaza, W. 34 St. off 7th Ave., 52nd St. off 6th Ave., W. 37th St. off 6th Ave.	15
Selected blocks between Houston and 14th Sts.			West End Ave. off 60th St. Selected blocks on and crossing Aves. A, B, C, D, off Ave. C.	11
9th Ave.	596–763 9th Ave.	W. 42nd to W. 52nd Sts.	8th Ave. off 43rd St.	11
Columbus Ave.	692–963 Columbus	W. 94 to W. 108th Sts.		6

QUEENS BLACKOUT AREAS

Commercial Strip	Strip Boundaries	Cross Streets	Stem Commercial	Number of Stores Affected
Jamaica Ave.	147–08 to 182–30 Jamaica	147th to 183rd Sts.	Scattered stores between Jamaica, N.Y. Blvd. and Merrick Blvd.	31
Queens Village	211–60 to 267–27 Hillside Ave.	211th to 267th Sts. Springfield Blvd. off	Hollis Ave. between 206th and 218th Sts.	11
So. Ozone Pk. Main St., Flushing	103-09 to 130–08 Roosevelt Ave. to 41st Rd.	103rd to 130th Sts.	113th St.	7 7

iii

THE STYLE OF THE LOOTING

In the rioting of the 1960s, the disorders often began as the result of a so-called "precipitating incident," which usually involved an altercation between the police and one or more citizens. Then a period of rage and chaos would follow, with ghetto residents throwing rocks and bottles at the police and other symbols of authority. In this first stage of the typical civil disturbance of the 1960s, little looting occurred. Instead destructive attacks were directed at objects symbolic of the underlying sources of conflict.

The second phase of the disturbances of the sixties included looting. Some violent attacks continued, but without the intensity of the earlier period. Black-owned stores containing choice merchandise were not automatically spared by the plundering looters. The racial dimension, write Dynes and Quarantelli, while not absent, appeared secondary to the economic factor.[1]

In the third stage of the sixties disturbances, there was a "full redefinition of certain property rights," and looting became a mass activity. The carnival spirit often described in the big-city riots of Newark and Detroit was, according to Dynes and Quarantelli, not representative of anarchy, but was an overt manifestation of general localized support for the new definition of property rights.[2] Looting was widespread and open, instead of stealthy, and people worked together in groups or family units.

In the disturbances of the 1960s, then, an orderly, focused search for goods and material grew out of an angry, chaotic racial attack on symbols of white authority.

In the 1977 blackout looting, as already noted, the stages were reversed. When the lights went out, the first stage began with hasty attacks on stores that had the best merchandise. This stage was dominated by criminals who applied a high level of sophistication to the task of getting the stores open. Where necessary, ten to fifteen people were marshaled to tear down steel gates protecting storefronts.

In the second stage of the blackout looting, large numbers of young people, roving bands of youths, brought a degree of confusion to the scene. But, one or two hours after the looting had begun there was still a considerable amount of cooperation.

In the third stage, the systematic, orderly looting gave way to hysteria. This was due partly to the large numbers of people in the streets, and also to the growing numbers of police on the scene making arrests and trying to wrest command of the area. Many people representing all economic and social classes were now participating. Mobs of youths still raced through the streets and occasionally threw rocks and bottles at the police. The earlier atmosphere of people cooperating with each other and sharing merchandise seemed to move into one in which people scuffled and fought for goods and appliances already taken from stores. Thus what had begun as a deliberate pursuit of goods initiated by the criminal class of the neighborhood, evolved into a disorganized, chaotic scramble for whatever was left, marked by only little evidence of racial rage and anger.

In Bushwick a youth worker, Aubrey Edmonds, was out that night, and he went up and down Broadway and watched what happened from the very beginning. He not only works in the community but lives half a block from Broadway. Judging from his relationship with locals as we walked along the street with him, he is extremely knowledgeable about what is going on in the area. He gave this account:

It was started by twenty-one to thirty-year-olds who knew what to get and where to get it. This was their business. It was a case of mostly everybody waiting for these people to do their thing—to do the initial break-in. They'd get thirty to forty hands on the gate and pull and pull. Pretty soon, it would come down. If it didn't come down, they'd take a rest, throw a few bottles around and then they'd go at it again. Pretty soon, it would pop, and they'd be in.

Aubrey said that in some instances the group would act like an army platoon, some grabbing the cash registers, others the shiniest merchandise. They would then run off and hit another store, leaving the first one open for everyone else to continue plundering.

In Harlem we heard similar reports. Mr. Greene, black manager of the Lehman Music Co. at 68 West 125th Street, tried to protect the store by staying in it that night. He said the stores he saw opened on 125th Street were hit by cohesive groups of young people. In some instances, he told us, they would even keep others out of the store while they went in and "got the stuff they wanted." In a similar incident at a liquor store on Reid Avenue at Madison Street in Bedford-Stuyvesant, the owner said his neighbors told him that several men clipped the locks off his gate with huge lock cutters, and then went in with guns drawn. "They held off the others in the street until they got the register and went through the store looking for money," he said.

"It was guys in their late twenties and thirties in the beginning, and the younger people, eighteen to nineteen, came in later," said Lt. Matthews of the 28th Precinct in Harlem. "The street people were the first ones out, and as it progressed later and later, others got involved. If you weren't criminally inclined, your first inclination that night was to go and see if your family was ok, and *then* go out on the street."

In East Harlem, Willie Stewart, deputy director of the East Harlem Community Corporation, was out that night keeping an eye out in general, and checking on a street gang his group is working with (he said those youths were not involved). "It was the junkie population that started it," he said. "One junkie would take a garbage can, throw it through the window, and then all the others would follow."

On Utica Avenue in Crown Heights, Reverend Clarence Norman of the First Baptist Church on Eastern Parkway said that roving bands would open one store after another, clean out what they wanted, and move on. Brother Ramzas, who is organizing a community police force called the "Red Jackets" to patrol Utica Avenue, agreed with the roving band theory; he also agreed with Reverend Norman that the early looters tended to be recent immigrants from rural areas of the Caribbean.

We found in interview after interview that all the big hits, which were on stores carrying expensive, easily fenceable merchandise, tended to come within the first hour and a half after the blackout. "From 9:30 to 11:00 P.M. was when all the major breaks had been made," said Sergeant Freud, the patrol supervisor of the 24th Precinct on the Upper West Side of Manhattan. He and others in the precinct characterized the rest of the evening as "scavenging."

"The real damage was done in a short period of time," said Captain O'Sullivan of the 77th Precinct in Bedford-Stuyvesant. "Once the extra units were on hand, the damage was already done."

As soon as the first stores were cracked open, word quickly spread about what was going on "down the avenue," "over on the boulevard," or wherever the shopping spine was; and the street people who dominated Stage II moved onto the scene in huge numbers. "The last blackout," said anticrime officer Adalto Lourenso of the Crown Heights precinct, "people didn't know what it was or how long it would last. This time when the lights stayed out for a while, they knew they weren't going to come on for a long time. So they said, 'Hey, I'm going and getting some stuff.' "

Because of the blackness, even a rough estimate of how many people were on any one street is only guesswork, but witness after witness said the numbers were truly awesome. On Utica Avenue in Crown Heights, the police estimated that "thousands" were crammed into a narrow street five blocks long. The people were impenetrable. Squad cars made no attempt to get through. The looters carried on with complete freedom.

Trying to characterize the conduct and make-up of those crowds is a futile project, for they varied with each block and changed as the evening wore on. From the fairly methodical opening of stores in the beginning, to the pitch of frenzy in Stage III, more and more people poured into the streets, and the police began to chase them up and down.

The crowds on Broadway in Bushwick seemed to possess a special kind of hysteria as the evening wore on. This spirit appeared to lead them as much toward destruction and burning as toward looting. "I found it hard to believe," says Captain Driscoll of the 81st Precinct in Bedford-Stuyvesant. He was down on Broadway that night, and thought the crowds were displaying a kind of madness. "They were like bluefish in a feeding frenzy . . . the strongest feeling I had was one of disbelief. I've seen looting before, but this was total devastation. Smashing, burning . . . as if they'd gone crazy."

Indeed, all the goods pouring out of stores and the people racing madly through the streets seemed to foment emotional outbursts that frightened even the looters themselves, who saw the situation getting out of control. The following is an excerpt from an interview with one male looter who was on Pitkin Avenue in Brownsville that night:

Looter: . . . You see, I mean, all the businesses that got torn up, most of them are back in business except for the ones that got burnt down which was really wrong, but like, people just couldn't, you know, nobody really thought about what they was doing. Everybody was lootin'. A lot of people was just outright—it was fucked up, the way they went about doing what they did, you know. 'Cause everybody could've come off and nobody didn't have to get hurt. If people woulda acted like they had a little bit of sense, act like some kind of self-control.

Interviewer: How do you figure they could do that?

Looter: Some people just don't give a fuck about other people. They don't give a damn. Some people was just out there being destructive. There was people out there just tearing up shit, just to be tearing up. I mean there were people out there doing it. Just tearin' up. Burning down stores and shit, you know, hurting people purposely. Some people were just out there for that purpose, just to be doin' stupid shit like that.

Interviewer: And you don't believe in that?

Looter: Naw, I mean I was out there 'cause I'm a poor person and like, you know, like a hungry dog meet up with some food, you know he gonna eat it, that's what a poor person is. I mean, when he sees a chance to get what he wants.

(As it turned out, this man didn't get all he wanted that night. On the way home from his third looting trip, carrying a television set, he was set upon by someone who came out of the darkness and struck him with a club, whereupon the looter dropped the TV set and ran home.)

While no valid generalization on looting behavior can be applied to all neighborhoods throughout the evening, there is little evidence to support an interpretation of the night as a "reign of terror." Most typical among eyewitness accounts were descriptions of the crowds as lacking menace and showing little hostility toward either the police or white store owners who stayed with their shops. "There was so much to steal that night," said the owner of a jewelry store at Fulton Street and Nostrand Avenue in Bedford-Stuyvesant, "that if the looters met even the slightest resistance in a store, they tended to go on to somewhere else."

It is remarkable, in fact, that out of all the black/white confrontations that were possible that night, virtually none materialized. Much credit for the lack of racial fighting has been given, deservedly so, to patrolmen for keeping their cool. But some credit belongs to the looters who engaged in very little of the traditional bottle-throwing and police-baiting that occurred in the riots of the 1960s. "It was clear they didn't want us," said one patrolman from the 83rd Precinct in Bushwick who was on Broadway that night. "If they'd wanted us, they could have had us anytime that night. There was nothing we could have done about it."

"We were just pests," said Sergeant O'Houlihan, patrol supervisor of the 73rd Precinct in Brownsville. "We were just something to get around so they could get at the goods." Captain O'Sullivan of the 77th Precinct in Bedford-Stuyvesant said with amazement that at one point during the looting, he and two policemen found themselves alone in the middle of a crowd of 150 looters and would-be looters, "and I never felt we were in danger of being attacked."

Even more surprising, when large numbers were arrested, the general lack of ill-will toward the police prevailed even though there was much more body contact than there had been in the riots a decade before. "It was almost a game," said one captain in the Bronx. "The men would grab some kid in a store, and he'd say, 'Okay you got me,' and go along quietly." During the blackout the police would wade into a street, grab looters by their limbs and clothing, and wrestle them into cars. By contrast, in the Harlem Riot of 1964, they stood aloof from the mobs and simply fired pistols into the air to chase crowds off the main street. And they ended up making few arrests. The close contact in the blackout looting, said Police Commissioner Codd, was the reason policemen suffered many more injuries such as cuts, sprains, bruises and broken limbs, than they did during the 1960s riots.

Some whites who saw the looting close up, of course, were understandably afraid. "We were terrified," said one of the two owners of Woman Books, a feminist bookstore at 92nd Street and Amsterdam. Both proprietors stayed in their store while a large furniture store was looted across the street. "The yelling, the breaking glass—it sounded really horrible." Yet for all the noise, in the one or two approaches would-be looters made at their door, it was enough for them only to shine a flashlight out from the interior to turn away potential intruders.

Watching essentially the same scene from the vantage point of the third floor in an apartment house overlooking Amsterdam Avenue at 92nd Street, Susan Feldstein, another white, said she was horrified at what was going on, but never felt it involved any anger directed at her as a white. "I always felt I could have gone out there, and no one would do anything to me, even though there were no whites there," she said. "I felt no one would harm me."

"In the 1972 riots in Brownsville* someone came at me with a hatchet," said Wayne Barrett, a research assistant for this report and a white resident of Brownsville. "During that riot, I was running. Even the cops were turning and running. But this time, I was coming down from a meeting onto Pitkin Avenue when the lights went out, and within five minutes there must have been 500 people on the street. But they weren't paying any attention to me; they were hitting the stores."

"The only thing that really surprised me," said Willis Barnes, the 31-year-old ex-convict we talked to while buildings still smouldered in Bushwick, "was that it was quite orderly. Usually in a thing like that you'd see people busting each other up and stomping each other. That night I didn't hear anyone say, 'Let's go mug somebody.'"

Looters also demonstrated little ill will toward each other. While some police did notice pulling and tugging over goods, especially as the easily lootable merchandise began to get scarce during Stage III, good humor seemed to last most of the night. And in several instances, the looting gave poor people a chance to experience the rare personal satisfaction derived from dispensing charity to others. "At some stores it was like a Robin Hood thing," said Patrolman Bruce Rivera of the 44th Precinct in the Highbridge section of the Bronx. "People would be grabbing stuff out of stores and passing it out to people on the street, just giving it to them."

Sometime after midnight, the Stage II looting population

---

*A localized disturbance growing out of a district school board election.

was enlarged by Stage III participants, the more stable poor and working class members of the community who were swept into the stealing. These were often the "mothers, fathers and children" that police reported seeing mostly in supermarkets, furniture stores or clothing shops. They accounted for most of the 1,000 people the police saw in an A&P on University Avenue in the Bronx at about 1:00 A.M. They were presumably heavily involved in the looting of furniture stores, acquiring things for their apartments. Ms. Batchelder of Woman Books, who watched the looting of the Capri Furniture store across Amsterdam Avenue, said she saw several instances of children and mothers carrying couches and other furniture around the corner to their apartments. It was undoubtedly a Stage III middle-aged man that Captain Driscoll saw run out of a store on Broadway in Bushwick with a large box, and feverishly open it to see what he had gotten, only to find that it contained several gross of clothespins.

For some of the Type III looters it seemed almost a matter of principle that they take something that night, even if it was something for which they had no use. "The next day," said one policeman from the 77th Precinct in Bedford-Stuyvesant, "we found a shopping cart standing on the sidewalk, and across the top was this huge, five-foot-long side of beef still mostly frozen. It was as if the guy who'd stolen it suddenly said to himself, 'What the hell am I doing with this?' and so he left it there."

By daylight the looting had lost its force. As of 5:30 A.M., the police had made a majority of the arrests they would make in the twenty-four hours following the blackout. In some areas, of course, the stealing persisted into the next day and evening. Again, this was particularly true in Bushwick, where in the confusion of fire trucks and the darkness caused by the elevated tracks, people had a few more hours to sift through the opened stores. On the Lower East Side, hardware-store owners alerted the 9th Precinct to the unusually high sales of lock cutters and hacksaw blades during the day. These items were presumably bought by people getting ready for another go-around that night should the lights fail to come on.

But for the most part the daylight looting consisted merely

of women and children gleaning through already thoroughly looted shopping streets for objects dropped or left behind. So it was that one old woman in East Harlem was found searching in the gutter outside a jewelry store for "joyas," or bits of jewelry she hoped the looters may have dropped in haste the night before.

iv

THE MERCHANTS

Of the 1,616 merchants whose stores were looted and/or damaged that night, the overwhelming majority, judging by the blackout loans given out by the Small Business Administration, were white and lived outside the neighborhood. Most, we have concluded from our own interviews, were from Rockland County, Queens or Long Island. Of the 535 SBA blackout loans, 387 went to whites, while only 80, or 15 percent, went to blacks, and 68, or 13 percent, went to Puerto Ricans.[1]

No estimate is available of how many store owners were completely driven out of business. Nevertheless, in ghetto neighborhoods the looting certainly decreased, for a time at least, the variety of goods available for sale, and it surely cut down on the already short supply of large supermarkets, in addition to the jobs available for clerks and stockboys. A more costly blow, according to Victor Marrero, was to shop-

ping streets in transitional neighborhoods such as Flatbush
and the upper Concourse in the Bronx, where merchants' re-
solve to stay in the inner city was shaky even before the lights
went out.

"It's especially depressing for people like myself," said
Dr. Ernest Zelnick, who runs the Professional Hearing Aid
Services at 705 Flatbush Avenue, and who suffered fire damage in apartments he owns above the store. "I'm on the planning board, past president of the Chamber of Commerce. I've
given my life for this community, trying to convince other
merchants to stay on, not to move down to Kings Plaza (a
large shopping mall at the southern end of Flatbush Avenue).
And here I get a call at 2:00 A.M. telling me there's looting,
and my building's burning."

Dr. Zelnick, who lives in the Mill Basin section of Flatbush near Kings Plaza, and who has been in business on Flatbush Avenue for thirty years, has repaired the damage to his
store and building and is not ready to move. His confidence in
the avenue, however, was severely shaken. "Would you want
your wife to come and shop in an area where there was looting
and burning?" he said. The fault that night, he thinks, lay
mostly with black leaders in the neighborhood who, in his
view, should have been out on the streets trying to stop the
looting. "We need more responsibility on the part of black
leaders," he said. "This is an integrated community. We all
get along fine, but I think the black clergy should have been
out that night trying to put a stop to it."

Whether black leadership could have done anything once
the hysteria loosed itself on the streets is doubtful. Evidence
from the kinds of stores hit that night shows that the crowds
were much less ready than they had been in the 1960s to be
swayed by someone merely because he was black and pro-
fessed identity with the plight of the poor.

In Bedford-Stuyvesant, Syl's Trophies and Sporting
Goods store on Nostrand Avenue at Park Street has been a local institution ever since it opened nine years ago. On its exterior walls is a mural depicting Hank Aaron, O. J. Simpson,
Arthur Ashe, Pele, and Martin Luther King, Jr., along with

Babe Ruth and John Kennedy. The owner, a talkative 41-year-old black named Syl Williamson, serves as a godfather to children in the neighborhood, helping them to start bank accounts, and advising them on college choices and career problems. He donates uniforms to four baseball teams. "Even the parents," said Mrs. Williamson, "come down to have Syl talk with their children when there are problems."

Along with instant lectures on self-help and the importance of moral and religious values, Williamson tries to give the community a good deal else. He is quick to point out that Pro-Ked sneakers selling for $15 in the big department stores in downtown Brooklyn go for $13.95 in his shop. "More is expected of a black store owner," he says. "You're expected to be more compassionate; you can't sell shoddy goods. And if a bill comes to $18.25, you're expected to forget the 25 cents."

The night of the blackout, however, he got a call that people were in his store, and by the time he got down there with his wife at 10:30 P.M., he was nearly cleaned out—a loss he estimates at about $140,000. He said he recognized some of the people as he grabbed frantically at the sporting goods they carried off. "But you don't really want to recognize them," he said. "They're the same ones who'll be shopping here, and you try to block it out of your mind."

His wife said she was so furious she wanted to "run them over with the car." Syl, however, is of a mind to forget it and get on with rebuilding his business. He blames the looting fever on the general decline of moral backbone in the black and white communities alike. "They looted the store because for twelve years they've been programmed to take, and that's where it's coming from," he said. "It's the news media and the social workers. We're getting away from the merit syndrome. There was a time a black had to be four times as good as everyone else to get something. Now, he thinks that just because he *is*, he gets it."

There was, of course, some indication of racial consciousness during the blackout. The black manager of a white-owned music store on 125th Street in Harlem told us of having a tug-of-war with a looter over a stereo set while the two argued over whether the store owner was white or black. In the end the stereo went the way of most other merchandise in the store, but it is not clear whether the manager's loss resulted from an unconvincing argument or inadequate strength.

In more typical instances, the looters saw only the value of merchandise and cared little for the color of its owner. Black stores were looted alongside those of whites if they, too, sold the main items on the looting list. This was particularly true of the black-owned stores which did a "high style" business, such as the LeMans clothing store on Amsterdam Avenue at 93rd Street, where customers are served wine and cheese while they scan the racks of expensive threads. The store was looted thoroughly and its interior ripped apart; owners could not reopen for eight months because they had had to make such extensive repairs.

For a black business to escape that night, it had to come up with the same kind of defense as the white businesses. Across from the Bedford-Stuyvesant Restoration Corporation, for instance, a black-owned tuxedo shop was broken into and the looters got away with what the owner said was one-third of his stock. His store might have been completely cleaned out had not the guards from the Restoration Corporation arrived to chase them off and keep the store under their protection for the rest of the night.

 On Broadway in Bushwick, the only one of four large markets that survived was one owned by a black. It escaped because the owner and his two brothers kept guard all night, armed with clubs and a dog. The owner also has a fairly formidable reputation. "The word in the street," says Capt. Driscoll of the nearby 81st Precinct, "is he'll do a real number on you if he catches you messing with his store."

In the more racially conscious rioting of the 1960s, the Fort Greene Cooperative Supermarket located on Myrtle Avenue in the Fort Greene section of Brooklyn would almost certainly have escaped damage. Begun as a community effort in 1974, the cooperative started with $130,000 in capital. After three years of struggle it employs 23 full- and part-time people and is finally seeing evidence of success. Its gross has risen steadily from $1.2 million to $3 million and, according to its chairman, Emile A. Curry, the enterprise had forecast a profit in 1977 for the first time.

The store benefits cooperative members by holding out the promise of a rebate if it goes into the black. But shoppers in general benefit from lower prices on canned goods, good-quality meat and produce at competitive prices, and what Mr. Curry described as a "fair and honest" attitude toward customers. "The people know that unlike the other markets, when they come here on check day, the prices won't go up," he said.

A less fortunate distinction, as far as the blackout went, was that, unlike a competing Finast market down the street, the cooperative had never bothered to install metal gates across its full-length plate glass windows. When the lights went out, Curry said, the store was broken into "within minutes." All the meat was taken as well as canned goods, beer and its cash registers—an $89,000 loss in all. At the nearby Finast, looters found the gates too tough to pry open and left it untouched.

"I thought we had deep roots in the community," Mr. Curry said, "but this kind of store is new to people, and I guess it will take more time."

One thing the looting made clear was that as minority groups begin to take over a significant number of businesses in the black community, they, like their white predecessors, increasingly fall victim to its crime. One merchant who said that crime along Broadway in Bushwick has virtually changed his personality was Luther Hawkin, a forty-one-year-old black pharmacist who for the last eight years has owned a drugstore on Broadway in Bushwick. A carefully dressed man with a quiet, precise way of expressing himself, Mr. Hawkin sold a smaller store in Crown Heights and bought his present place in 1970 from two whites who left to open a store on Long Island. He had a partner then, a white man, who sold out his share of the business a year later when thieves, in a final affront, stripped his car while it was parked only fifty yards from the store. "I was never angry at him for leaving," says Mr. Hawkin, who earned his degree from the Brooklyn College of Pharmacy. "It was too much to ask of a human being to stay."

Since then, Mr. Hawkin has stayed on, although the business has declined slowly and steadily. Whereas in 1973 the store had nine employees, including three pharmacists, it is now down to four, including the owner. This, however, doesn't bother him as much as the steady drumbeat of crime. His store is broken into regularly, five or six times a year. They come up through the floor, through the cellar door, in the back door, through the back wall, down through the roof. Next door, they tunneled through a brick wall merely to get at a cleaning establishment. "It's unreal," he said.

There are literally fist fights in the store, the use of weapons, the use of clubs. I had to learn to deal with the element in a way they required. I don't say it proudly. I have children and I try to raise them decently. I go to church. I don't like doing it, but it's a must. In order to stay on in this corner, it was a simple must. If you capitulate, forget it, they'll walk right over you.

Mr. Hawkin carries a pistol, and once, two years ago, he shot a burglar. It was late at night, when he was doing accounts. Two men came in through the rear. He fired at them and they ran off. He saw blood on the ground but doesn't know how badly the person was wounded. "My family doesn't recognize me anymore," he said. "I find myself swearing as I do in the store, and I have to stop and see that I'm home."

The night of the looting, Mr. Hawkin was on his way home to Crown Heights. When the lights went out, he turned his car around, went back to his store, and stayed there, holding his gun, through the night and into the next day. His place was untouched until 4:00 P.M. on July 14th, when he left for half an hour to eat. Within minutes looters broke in his side windows and started to take watches, pocketbooks and cologne.

When he returned it was too late; they had already stolen most of his merchandise. They dispersed only after he fired a shot over their heads.

While crime in the ghetto is hardly an unreported phenomenon, the effect it has on the conduct of business is hard to appreciate unless one spends time in shops and listens to merchants talk about their lives behind the counter. Jack Weinstein, 57, typical of the dozens we interviewed, owns Jack's Bargain Store, an Army/Navy clothing and accessory store at 1439 Fulton Street in Bedford-Stuyvesant.

Mr. Weinstein, who opened the store in 1945, was home in Rosedale, Queens, that night. He got a call at 11:00 A.M. that his store had been looted. Now he cannot talk about the $20,000 loss without "getting a headache." The looters that night came in through a door in the rear, an egress he promptly closed with cinder blocks and cement. Then, five times in quick succession, burglars came in through the roof in September, October and November. To stop this, Mr. Weinstein is having 12-by-2-inch beams laid like planks across the roof and fastened with eight-inch spikes. As added protection, at night he takes most of his merchandise off the racks and locks it away in footlockers hidden in a storage room on the side of the store.

"You go to the cops, and ask them what to do and they say 'Sleep in the store,'" he said. "Sure, 'sleep in the store.' Then they come in and kill you! 'Get a dog,' they say, 'get a dog.' They spray the dogs and come in anyway; big deal! They're not afraid of the dogs. Tell about the dogs to the fifteen- to seventeen-year-old kids who need ready cash and got no jobs."

Ghetto merchants continue to tolerate such an existence in some cases because they are too old and undercapitalized to move their businesses to a safer area. In other instances, however, their tenacity can be taken as powerful evidence that a significant amount of money is still to be made in poor neighborhoods.

Up the block from Jack's, the Fulton Pawnbrokers at 1543

Fulton Street also claimed a loss of $20,000 in merchandise that night. Because of precautions taken since the blackout, the shop now seems capable of defying anything less than a wheelbarrel full of dynamite. The owner simply filled in his two display windows with cement, so customers must pass through a bunkerlike hallway to get to his front door. To house the pledges brought in by what seems to be a steady stream of customers, he had already constructed a block-house at the rear of his store, which is completely encased in cinder blocks except for a small doorway to the interior of his shop. The exact value of goods stored in the stronghold is a matter "between me and Dun and Bradstreet," he said.

Lester Shaw, the owner of a pawn shop on 125th Street in Harlem, was less hesitant to discuss his business, which seems to add up to a considerable enterprise. A long-retired New York City policeman, Mr. Shaw opened for business twenty-two years ago, and until the looting had never suffered a serious robbery or burglary. This immunity from crime was despite—or possibly because of—the fact that the store is located literally in a den of thieves. Overhead is a brothel; prostitutes work on the street corner; pimps and junkies perambulate day and night. Within a long stone's throw are three methadone clinics. The block on which the store is located is so crime-ridden that most of the storeowners there have boarded up and left.

At 7:30 on the morning after the blackout, Mr. Shaw received a call at his home in Rockland County from his son who had come down to open the store. "My god, Dad," the son said, "we've been wiped out."

After prying up the sheathing the looters got one of the biggest hauls in the city that night, including 175 television sets and numerous fur coats, record players, musical instruments, appliances, cameras and other merchandise, most of it stored in three tiers of racks in a second-floor warehouse. All they left was a pile of golf clubs in the middle of the floor.

In all, Mr. Shaw reported a loss to the police and the insurance company of $275,000. But this, as it turns out, wasn't half of what he had on hand. Looters tried to get into three huge safes at the back of the store but gave up after they had only knocked off the handles. Mr. Shaw uses the safes to store small pledges such as jewelry and watches left by customers to be held against loans. He said he values these pledges at $330,000.

THE POLICE RESPONSE

As the looter and the looting seemed to fall into three general, if overlapping, stages of development, so too were there different and distinct levels of police response, depending on the time of night. The first level lasted two to three hours after the lights went out. During this time, the police lacked manpower and could do little but chase people relatively harmlessly around the precincts. The second level of response began at about 12:30 A.M.. It was then the police started making a significant number of arrests.

Examining the ways in which the two levels of police response interlaced with the stages of looting, we arrived at two conclusions: first, the spontaneity in the outbreak of looting together with the absence of strong initial police action created a feeling among the looters and would-be looters alike that they were immune from arrest. This sense that they would suffer few or no consequences as a result of their actions was responsible in large part for the build-up of a tremendous momentum in the looting, to the point at which it could only have been stopped by huge masses of men. As Capt. O'Sullivan of the 77th Precinct in Bedford-Stuyvesant said: "By the time we got enough men to do anything that night, it was already too late."

We also concluded that the delay in making arrests until the early hours of the morning meant generally that those who profited most from the looting stood the last chance of going to jail. The peak period for arrests was between 1:30 and 2:30 A.M., which corresponds to the time when the greatest number of Stage II and Stage III looters were on the streets.[1] During the lowest period for arrests, in the hours immediately following the blackout, the Stage I looters seem to have been most heavily involved. From 9:35 P.M. to 12:30 A.M., which is when almost all the stores were opened up and the cream of the goods stolen, the police made only 7 percent of the total number of blackout arrests.

Merchants were quick to criticize the police, despite their lack of numbers, for not being more aggressive toward the early looters and, in particular, for not "shooting to kill," a policy which many merchants felt might have stemmed the stealing and about which we will have more to say later. It is interesting to note that this criticism of "being soft" came as routinely as did the charges ten years ago of "police brutality," which were leveled by minority-group leaders who felt the police lad overreacted in many instances during the riots.

Whatever the merits of either charge, they suggest what a distance the country has come in the intervening years. They also illustrate the dilemma faced today by beat patrolmen who are slowly being ground down by the frustration they feel from continually being "damned if they do and damned if they don't."

In any event, judging from the testimony of all the experts we interviewed, it seems plain that the high degree of self-control exhibited by the police under very difficult circumstances can be credited with staving off a far worse explosion than the one that erupted. Not one rioter was shot by the police, although two were killed by storeowners. In fact, since there was generally strict adherence by the police to departmental regulations concerning random shooting, very few shots came from the police at all during the night.[2] Many community people, who normally are loath to give the police credit for anything, remarked repeatedly about the police cool.

While, on the other side, patrolmen disagreed among themselves over the no-shooting policy, a majority seemed to think it made eminent sense. "If we'd have shot just one person that night," said an officer who was in the midst of the fray on Broadway in Brooklyn, "we'd have had a war on our hands."

* * *

Never in history have all of New York's five boroughs been simultaneously involved in a civil disorder, and it was alarming indeed to see how thin was the blue line when it was stretched so tight. "The whole strategy during disorders," says Capt. O'Sullivan of Bed-Stuy's 77th Precinct, "is to move men from where you don't need them to areas where you do need them. We can get anywhere from 100 to 1,000 men to a trouble spot in pretty quick time. But there's nothing you can do if it goes up everywhere at once." During the Harlem riots in 1964, recalls Captain Baker of the 67th Precinct in Flatbush, hundreds of men were sent into Harlem, but this left some precincts in the Bronx with "one patrol car each," which would hardly have been enough to contain any trouble had it erupted there, too.

As for what to do if the whole city is enveloped by disorder at once, the police department has no general, effective policy. "If we had any policy for what we were supposed to do in a blackout like this," says a sergeant who served as a patrol supervisor in Brooklyn, "I didn't know about it."

When the looting broke out along Broadway in Bushwick, the 83rd Precinct, which covers the community of 90,000 inhabitants, had only 14 men in seven patrol cars out on the streets. To cover Bedford-Stuyvesant, the 77th, 79th and 81st

Precincts had 73 men among them, and the 81st had most of its men tied up on Broadway, which it covers together with the 83rd in Bushwick. In all the Brooklyn North Command, which covers Williamsburg, Bushwick, Bedford-Stuyvesant, Ocean Hill, Brownsville, Crown Heights and East New York, only 189 men were on duty when the lights went out—this for a community of nearly 1,000,000 people, or enough to fill a city more than one and a half times the size of Boston.

As outlined in the typically understated manner of police jargon, here was the situation as defined by the ''critique,'' or self-analysis of the police response that evening. This statement was issued by the Brooklyn North Commander:

At the outset of the blackout, the widely dispersed activities of those involved in criminality made it virtually impossible to prevent individual acts of vandalism and looting. The vast number of individuals involved required personnel in excess of the number assigned to duty on the third platoon.[3]

A similar situation existed in the Bronx, where only 86 patrol cars and 6 foot-patrolmen were available for the whole borough, whose population is 1,380,000. In the words of Captain Gallagher of the 44th Precinct in Highbridge, which had to cope not only with a sizeable proportion of the borough's looting but also with a prison riot at the Bronx House of Detention:

At the time of the blackout there were 38 police officers on patrol. Ten times that number would have been necessary to cope with the spontaneous incidents of looting, fires, and attacks on police officers. The problem was not in the actions of the officers but in the fact that their number was insufficient.[4]

Graph V-1 displays the number of officers on patrol from the start of the blackout through midnight of the following day. According to the police log, there were 3,428 officers and detectives on patrol throughout New York City at 9:30 P.M. (2130) on July 13. Although police strength increased sharply within the first two and a half hours of the blackout, it was not until noon on July 14 that maximum strength was reached.

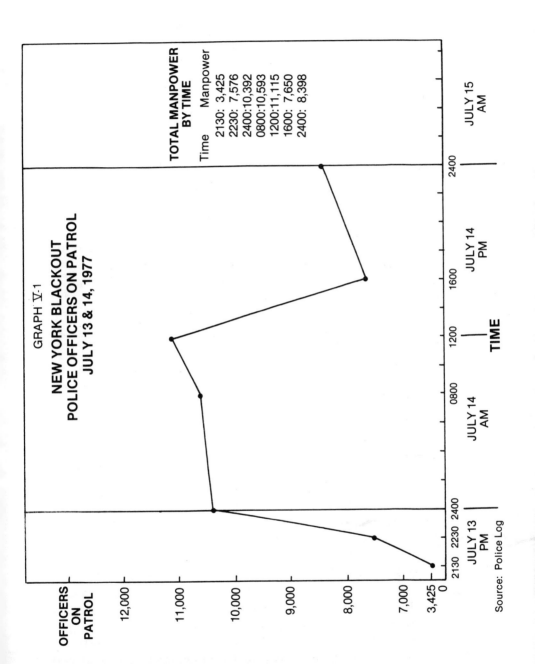

GRAPH Ⅴ-1
NEW YORK BLACKOUT
POLICE OFFICERS ON PATROL
JULY 13 & 14, 1977

TOTAL MANPOWER
BY TIME

Time	Manpower
2130:	3,425
2230:	7,576
2400:	10,392
0800:	10,593
1200:	11,115
1600:	7,650
2400:	8,398

OFFICERS
ON
PATROL

12,000
11,000
10,000
9,000
8,000
7,000
3,425
0

2130 2230 2400

JULY 13
PM

0800

JULY 14
AM

1200

TIME

1600

JULY 14
PM

2400

JULY 15
AM

Source: Police Log

Not surprisingly, the police could not react to the looting as they would have had they had enough men. That would have involved forming echelons one, two or three lines deep, sweeping through blocks to clean them of looters, and then leaving men behind to make blocks secure. Some echelons are V-shaped, spearheading into crowds to break them up. Sometimes they are flatfronted and porous, allowing some crowd members to pass through the echelon to be rounded up by back-up units operating in the rear. In either event, between 75 and 100 men would be needed to sweep a single block, according to Sgt. Floria of the 73rd Precinct in Brownsville. This was three or four times as many men as he had on hand that night for the entire precinct.

As it was, the police used a variety of tactics, with varying results. Four-man patrol cars, with two men staying behind at the scene of the looting, were used by the 25th Precinct in East Harlem. However, according to the precinct report, "it soon became obvious that bands of looters would retreat to adjacent side streets and wait until the officers were drawn to another involved store."[5]

Other precincts used four-man patrol cars to aid in making arrests, but no officers stayed behind.[6] Although this increased the number of arrests, it made it more difficult to transport prisoners and looted merchandise to the precincts, since there was less space in the patrol car. Some of the tactics changed with the police's perception of the nature of the looters. In the early hours in Flatbush, according to Captain Baker of the 67th Precinct, his men tended to travel in bunches for their own protection, leaving large numbers of stores unguarded. "Later," he said, "when they discovered that the crowds were not attacking them, they spread out a little."

One of the more effective strategies involved entering a heavily looted block from both ends to catch looters in the middle in a pincer movement made up of patrol cars and wagons packed with as many as twenty men. Using such a tactic, the 25th Precinct made eight arrests on two separate occasions. The arrests, however, were made at 2:45 A.M. and 3:00

A.M., which gave them little deterrent value. Generally precincts did not have enough men for such a maneuver, anyway. Some did not have sufficient men to make any arrests at all, for they feared that the bookkeeping involved in arrests would strip the streets of police. "Arrests were not warranted," said the official critique from the Brooklyn North Command, "due to the situation at hand where an arrest would take a police officer away from the area and reduce police personnel."[7]

The police department had had the foresight to equip precincts with Polaroid cameras, thereby enabling a clerk quickly to snap a picture of the patrolman together with the arrestee, so that the officer could get back on the streets. The paperwork could be done later. Success in putting the system to work, however, was decidedly uneven. Some precincts had cameras, but no film. Some had cameras locked in a closet, and no one could find a key. In some instances the cameras wouldn't work; in others, they just ran out of film. Police in one precinct forgot they had the camera in the first place.

The alternative to arresting was simply to chase. "In the beginning we attempted to chase people with cars," said Chief Bracey of Brooklyn North. "But seeing this, they became like flies in a kitchen; you hit over here, and they move over there. . . . We never got to the point where we could have a strategy. The only strategy was to try to pick up those who persisted, the ones who came back and back."

Sometimes the looters were so thick that the police couldn't even chase them. As noted earlier, the 71st Precinct in Crown Heights reported that the crowds on Utica Avenue were virtually impenetrable by squad car, stretching solidly from stores on one side of the street to those on the other.

"What you did? You did nothing," said Chief McDermott of the Bronx command. "All we tried to do was to maintain a strike force and concentrate it on priority runs like a 10-13 (patrolman needs assistance) or a robbery call." Arrests early in the evening were made only if policemen couldn't possibly avoid them. Sergeant Freud, patrol supervisor of the 24th Precinct on the Upper West Side of Manhattan, said his men en-

tered one man coming out of a liquor store, ordered him
ɔp the three bottles he was carrying and "take a walk." It
was only when the man refused to give up the liquor that the
policemen relented and placed him under arrest, Sergeant
Freud said.

Said Sergeant O'Houlihan, patrol supervisor of the 73rd
Precinct in Brownsville that night: "I told the cops to concentrate on prevention, on preventing looting, the form being to
make a lot of noise, drive the cars on sidewalks with sirens going and the lights on, to give the impression there were more
of us than there actually were. 'Make arrests,' I said, 'only
when necessary, only when you can't scare them away.' "

As a result the looters remained almost free from arrest in
the first three hours after the blackout. When Captain Gallagher arrived at the 44th Precinct in the Highbridge section of
the Bronx at 11:30 P.M., he found his men had made only one
arrest even though the streets of his precinct teemed with
looters. Men of the 81st Precinct in Bedford-Stuyvesant, who
helped the 83rd Precinct in Bushwick cover Broadway that
night, had managed to arrest only four people by 1:30 A.M.
This was four hours after the blackout had begun and long after much of the looting along Broadway had occurred. In
Crown Heights, Met Radio, a television and stereo store on
the corner of Utica Avenue and Eastern Parkway, reported a
loss that night of $300,000 in merchandise, the store's entire
stock. Yet police arrested only one person for looting at the
store, and he was accused of stealing a black-and-white TV
set.

"At 11:00 that night," said Sergeant O'Houlihan of the
Brownsville precinct, whose first arrest was made at 12:15
A.M., "we were letting the same guy go that we'd be arresting
later on at 12:30 in the morning."

Graph V-2 illustrates the number of arrests made hourly
from the start of the blackout until midnight of July 15th for
six precincts that experienced heavy looting. As we might expect, the greatest number of arrests were made during the period of greatest police strength, between 12:00 midnight July
13 and 6:30 the following morning. It is interesting to note that

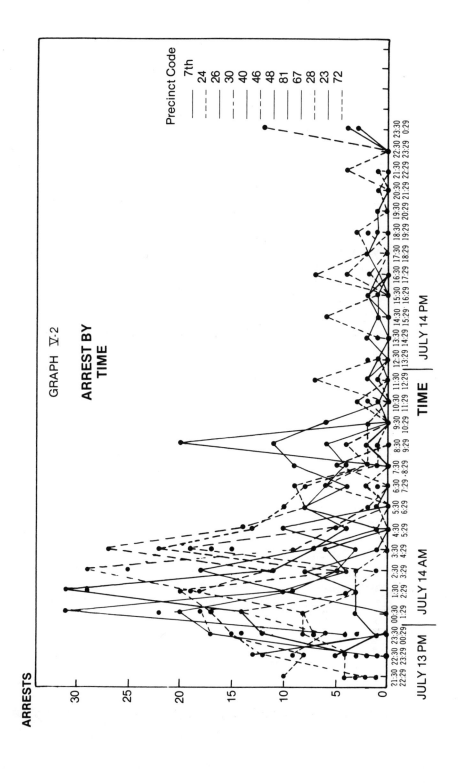

ARRESTS

GRAPH Ⅴ·2

ARREST BY
TIME

Precinct Code

7th
24
26
30
40
46
48
81
67
28
23
72

TIME

JULY 13 PM | JULY 14 AM | JULY 14 PM

the most sustained level of arrests was in the 48th Precinct in the Bronx, the third highest number of arrests was in the 46th Precinct, also in the Bronx, and the sharpest increase in the number arrested was in the 67th Precinct in Flatbush. If we examine the figures in the change (Δ) column in Table V-1, we see that for the precincts indicated on Graph V-2, the 46th, and 67th Precincts experienced the greatest increase of personnel during the period of their highest number of arrests. This relationship between manpower and the number of arrests made can be seen on Graph V-3.[8] The number of total hourly arrests for twelve precincts in New York City are presented on Graph V-4.[9]

Table V-1
OFFICERS ON DUTY BY PRECINCT AND TIME

Location & Precinct	Officers on Duty	July 13 2130–2400	+	July 14 0001–0800	+	0801–1600	+
Bushwick							
81	25	36	+11	49	+13		
83	26	70	+44	93	+23		
Bed-Stuy							
77	38	100	+62	192	+92	132	−60
79	28	68	+40	83	+15		
Brownsville							
73	27	93	+66	137	+44		
Flatbus ʰ							
67	21	67	+46	319	+252	339	+20
Crown Hts							
71	27	136	+109 +	434	+298	477	+43
Upper West Side							
24	25	101	+76	182	+81	216	+34
Harlem							
28	37	70	+33	92	+22	136	+44
E. Harlem							
25	47	137	+90	262	+145	327	+65
Morrisania							
48	37	140	+103 +	305	+165	195	−110

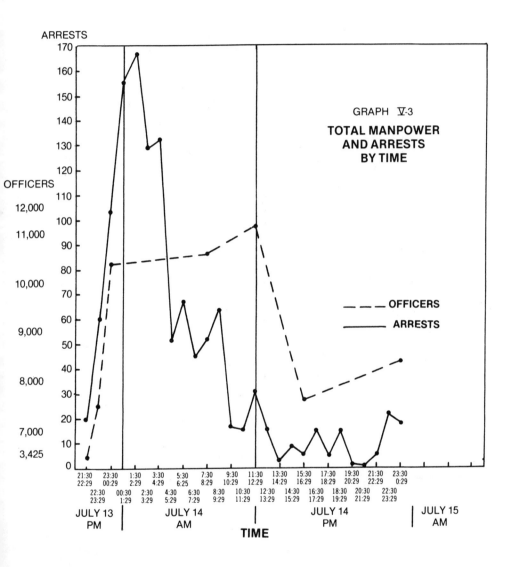

ARRESTS

GRAPH Ⅴ-3

**TOTAL MANPOWER
AND ARRESTS
BY TIME**

OFFICERS

– – – OFFICERS
——— ARRESTS

TIME

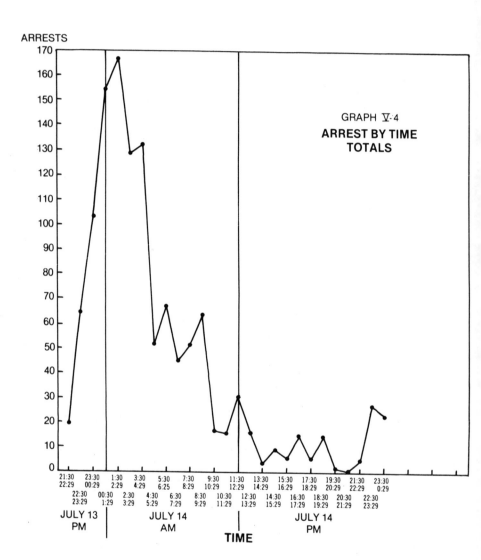

ARRESTS

GRAPH V-4
**ARREST BY TIME
TOTALS**

Since there may be a good deal of speculation involved in trying to explain why the number of arrests fall into so many peaks and valleys, we need to know how many looters were involved at any given time, rather than just the number of officers. We would also have to study the geographic layout of the precinct, the relation of command post to looted areas, and the number of areas affected.

Added to the initial manpower shortage, the department had considerable logistical problems bringing its off-duty policemen in from where they lived. Nearly half of the 8,000 off-duty policemen who reported that night had to come in from out of town; a majority of the others lived in Queens or Staten Island, far from the affected areas. The problem caused by their remoteness from the ghetto precincts was compounded by the nature of Commissioner Codd's call-up order, which sent the men to the precincts nearest their homes instead of the stationhouses where they normally worked. For one thing, this gave Queens, Staten Island and the North Bronx, where there was little looting, a preponderance of policemen. Captain Caputo of the 50th Precinct in Riverdale noted that members of the force were "responding more readily to 'quiet' commands." (Most of the arrests in Queens, unlike those in other boroughs, took place before midnight, and could well have been one important factor in stemming the looting in Jamaica.) Another problem resulting from Commissioner Codd's order was that because the men had not initially reported to their home precincts where all the riot gear was stored,* they showed up in the precincts without sticks, helmets or extra ammunition, and were ill-prepared to be of any real use. "I was overjoyed to hear I was getting a busload of guys from Staten Island," said Captain Driscoll in the beleaguered 81st Precinct. "But when they walked in the door, they looked like a tennis team." Near Fordham Road in the Central Bronx, one merchant reported seeing a policeman try to corral looters while he brandished a toilet bowl brush.

---

*This policy has since been changed, so that some men would now show up at prearranged check points where special gear has been stored.

Arriving generally without their uniforms, the out-of-precinct officers were also hard to identify as policemen. "In the absence of light, identification as police officers by shield alone is conducive to misunderstanding, confusion and error which may tend to make police control of the situation more difficult," read one police critique.[10]

The manpower problems were compounded by a communication failure caused by the blackout. Generators in many precincts, particularly in the Bronx and Brooklyn, had not been used extensively since their installation after the 1965 blackout, and in many cases they failed to work. In general precinct commanders said they had followed departmental policy of testing the generators at least once a month, but the brief tests did not determine whether the motors would work under intensive use. Generator failures not only made several police stations as dark as everywhere else, but left powerless the precinct gas pumps needed to keep patrol cars on the road all night. They also caused critical failures in the transmission boosters and "repeaters" needed to bring "911" calls into the precinct and to connect foot-patrolmen, who had walkie-talkies, to the precinct house. In Harlem and the Bronx, technicians managed to repair broken generators only to discover that roof antennas had never been hooked into the emergency transmission equipment powered by the generators. Communications in the Bronx were so fouled up that at one point during the prison eruption at the Bronx House of Detention, Chief McDermott was trying to find a pay phone so he could tell Corrections Commissioner Malcolm what was going on. "The breakdown in radio communication . . . denied necessary tactical information to those in command status," his critique later noted. "Thus police action for a time became fragmentary . . . Relay stations were down, therefore communications became virtually non-existent between various commands."[11]

The communications failure was not all bad. Several commanders said that with their cars unable to receive "911" calls, the precinct commanders themselves had the power to organize the defense of their own precincts rather than "losing'' cars to calls from central headquarters, since those calls might be of low priority.

Another aspect of police conduct which affected the extent of the looting was the generally strict adherence to departmental regulations that prohibit firing revolvers unless someone's life (including a policeman's) is in danger. The NYPD regulation in this regard goes even further than state law, which permits policemen to shoot at those fleeing the suspected commission of certain kinds of felonies. Any shooting incident must pass through an elaborate examination by the Weapons Discharge Review Board along with other layers of official inquiry. Whatever effect this screening has had in preventing innocent people from getting shot, there is little doubt that it makes a policeman think twice about casual shooting. Chief Bracey in Brooklyn said the system has reduced instances of shooting in his command from 67 in 1973 to 47 in 1976, and down to 43 in 1977. The attitude of the department was discussed in its critique by the Brooklyn North Area Task Force.

The Department's progressive philosophy is one that clearly delineates the fact that property rights are subservient to the right to life. Therefore, if life is not endangered legal force must be confined to other than lethal methods.[12]

And instructions issued to the men during the night of the blackout were explicit. This is from the commander's report in the 25th Precinct in East Harlem:

Due to the nature and relatively short duration of the emergency, printed instructions were not prepared. Verbal instructions were disseminated to all ranking officers and to all officers assigned through the 25th Precinct.

These instructions directed that officers use whatever means necessary, short of excessive and deadly force, to terminate and prevent looting, and to effect arrests of those committing such crimes. Confrontation which might escalate the situation was to be avoided, if possible, but not at the expense of presenting an image of the Department depicting officers standing by passively while stores were looted.

Firearms were only to be used as a last resort to protect police and civilians from deadly physical force. They were not to be used to protect property.[13]

A week after the blackout, the Police Department admitted officially to only two shooting incidents by policemen: in one, a revolver went off accidentally on Staten Island; the second involved a sergeant shooting a looter's dog in Queens. Our cursory examination of police reports turned up at least two more. One involved a patrolman in the Bronx who was shot in the leg by a sniper and then fired four shots into a crowd, apparently hitting no one. The other took place in Flatbush, where policemen fired ten shots into the air in what the captain there said was a conglomerate effort to scare off a sniper on a roof, discourage people from throwing down bottles, and protect the police themselves from a hostile crowd. Generally, though, the department policy on firing aimlessly into the air is almost as strict as it is against firing at people. In the first place, shots in the air can be dangerous, said Chief of Operations James F. Hannon. He cited an incident in which a patrolman, backed up against a wall by a crowd, fired into the air and hit a woman leaning out of a window above him. Secondly, he said, it can make the situation even more unmanageable. "What happens if you're firing in the air, but the people don't stop what they're doing? Do you then lower your gun and shoot them? And if they see you're not going to really shoot them, they know it's all a bluff, and you've landed yourself in a worse situation which it's hard to get out of."

This general police restraint—caused on the one hand by manpower shortages and logistics, and on the other by a conscious effort not to shoot people—had two general effects. On the positive side, it clearly prevented the looting from escalating into a disorder involving serious violence. On the other hand, the lack of shooting, combined with the low number of arrests, was seen by looters and people just hanging out on the street as evidence that they had license that night to do whatever they wanted without any recriminations. "The people on the street are pretty sophisticated about these things," said Chief Bracey. "They knew they weren't going to get shot, and the cops lived up to their expectations and didn't shoot . . . They also saw they were just getting chased . . . Cops didn't use excessive force, so they knew they weren't going to get a 'turbin' [police parlance for a bloodied head wrapped with a bandage]. There was no fear of any immediate punishment or future punishment either."

The pressing questions remains: What might the police have done that night? Clearly they could have used more men. But how many? At the onset of looting, the 28th Precinct in Harlem had three times its normal number of men.* Still it was unable to prevent much of the stealing. Maintaining the size of a police force that could deal effectively with such an outbreak would be, as Captain Brian Lavin of the 48th Precinct in the Bronx noted, extremely expensive.

Consideration of what might have been had we greater numbers of men and equipment can be taken only so far. The social and economic costs of maintaining a force of sufficient size to have fully coped with the myriad police related problems confronted during this emergency are clearly prohibitive.[14]

Some have offered suggestions for dealing with the looters that included calling in the National Guard, using massive doses of tear gas, bringing in large vans for mass arrests, and using fire department hoses as weapons to clear the streets of people.

The idea put forth most often that night was that the mayor should have asked the governor to send in the National Guard to help the police patrol looting areas.[15] The proposal was most strongly supported early in the morning of the day after the blackout by merchants and community people who, at the request of Mayor Beame, had been rounded up by police in each critical precinct and brought to City Hall for a meeting.

The decision not to request the Guard was made for several reasons. (The argument seems to have been moot anyway,

---

*This, as we shall detail later, was due to the presence of a fifty-three-man special drug-enforcement detail.

since Governor Carey has since said he would have refused to send in the Guard even if it had been requested.) For one thing, by the time the Guard could have been mobilized and transported into the city in significant numbers, it would already have been too late. "The critical time in these things is the first day—really, the first few hours," said Chief Hannon. To get the first units of the Guard on the street, however, would have taken at least eight hours, which was long after the bulk of the looting had taken place.

A more important consideration at City Hall that day was the Guard's general lack of preparedness for dealing with large urban disorders. The memory most alive in officials' minds concerned the Guard's dismal performance during the Newark Riots in 1967. Subsequent investigators concluded that the Guard had prolonged and exacerbated the violence. Not only are Guard units overwhelmingly white, but they are composed in large part of suburbanites and residents of small towns who have little or no familiarity with inner-city neighborhoods or minority groups. Because of this, the police and other officials felt, Guardsmen would have had a high propensity to panic. Panic among Guardsmen holding rifles might well have led to shooting, and shooting that night, according to virtually everyone we talked to, would have made matters much worse.

While most of the second-guessing has focused on the problems Guardsmen might have had with city residents, Dennis Wenger, writing in *The American Behavioral Scientist*, has examined the difficulties between Guardsmen and police officers that emerge in times of civil disturbances.

The relationship between the police and the national guard is structurally conducive to interorganizational conflict. Although cooperation and integrated activity can be observed in many situations, this relationship entails inherent difficulties concerning command, tactics, and operations. Furthermore, these difficulties are compounded by incompatible communications facilities between the organizations . . . Also, neither organization is quick to relinquish command over its operations.

. . . the two organizations . . . lack a basic knowledge of their counterpart's operational structure. The operational terminology of the two agencies is not similar. Confusion and misunderstanding often result in efforts at integrated action. Because the police do not function in a military manner during their normal operations, the issue is complicated. At the operations level, individual police officers are often assigned to work with from two to over ten guardsmen. The police, socialized toward autonomous and independent action, are likely not to understand the delay in military action. Conflict is likely to develop over the military's refusal to act without specific instructions. At the command level, conflicts over the use of force, manpower, and particularly tactical operations are likely to occur.[16]

What is more, to control such widespread disorders in New York without shooting—i.e., by sheer force of numbers—would have required an inordinately large Guard contingent. "People forget that New York is not like other cities, where you can just go in and smother the population," said Nicholas Scoppetta, the then Deputy Mayor for Criminal Justice who sat in on the City Hall meeting that morning. "Here, you can't just bring in a superior force big enough to overwhelm the population, even if it's only in one borough. There are just too many people."

For a number of reasons, therefore, it was decided that the dangers of calling in the Guard outweighed the possible benefits, and that the city would continue to rely on its smaller but street-smart police force which, by the morning at least, seemed to be muddling through.

Among the other ideas, tear gas was also considered—and rejected. The NYPD has never relied heavily on tear gas, Chief Hannon said, because it is uncontrollable. Fumes easily sift into residential areas, which could bring even more people out on the street; or they blow back on the police themselves, which would actually help the looters. Tear gas grenades are also a significant fire hazard.

Another idea propounded at the meeting was to bring in large vans and make sweeps of the streets; that is, mass arrests. For one thing, to have done this early in the evening, when it might well have had significant deterrent effect, required more men than the police had on duty. For another, using mass arrests as a tactic of breaking up crowds has been se-

verely criticized in police circles ever since the unfortunate
experience of the Washington, D.C., police department in
1971 when it used the tactic to clear peace demonstrators out
of the Washington Mall. Subsequent lawsuits by the ACLU
charging that the arrests without specific charges were a clear
abridgement of constitutional rights cost the municipality
$10,000 per arrest in damages and made a deep impression on
police commanders in New York. "Our policy is to make
'good' arrests," said Captain Baker of the 67th Precinct in
Flatbush. "You have to arrest people for committing a particular crime, and you have to have the evidence. We don't
make mass arrests."

Police commanders also rejected the idea of calling in the
Fire Department to wash looters off the street with high pressure hoses. In the first place, firemen had their hands filled
that night with fighting fires. Second, the NYFD went to a
great deal of trouble in the 1960s to project an image of help-
fulness and friendliness in minority neighborhoods in order to
convince young people not to throw bottles and rocks at
speeding fire engines. Signs were put on fire houses that re-
minded people: "We fight fires, not people."* To turn their
hoses on people during the looting would presumably have set
back their efforts considerably.

The police did call in members of the Auxiliary Police that
night and gave them ancillary duties, such as directing traffic
and providing information to people who showed up at precinct houses. The confidence in the effectiveness of Auxil-
iaries is so low among police commanders, however, that the
idea of sending them into looting areas was not even considered. "Mostly," said one sergeant of the 71st Precinct in
Crown Heights, which used thirty to forty auxiliary policemen that night, "we just had to make sure they didn't get
themselves hurt."

As shocking and, indeed, frightening as it was, the impo-
tence of the police that night only confirms the results of sev-

---

*These signs, incidentally, greatly miffed police officials who read them as an ac-
cusation that police *did* fight people, hardly the image they wished to project during
the racially sensitive years of the late 1960s and early 1970s.

eral studies which show how impossible is the task of control-
ling people who do not consent to be controlled, unless force
is used in utterly massive proportions.[17] That even large displays of force are sometimes unsuccessful was evident by the
inability of the police to keep thousands of fans, many of
them suburbanites, from swarming onto the field of Yankee
Stadium after the last game of the 1977 World Series.

vi

THE POLICE, THE
PEOPLE AND CRIME

It is not the purpose of this book to discuss in general the problems of law enforcement in poor neighborhoods, but as we drove around these areas with policemen and talked with their residents, it was impossible not to see patterns in police/community relations which affected the behavior of both groups during the night of looting.

For one thing, it is fairly obvious, even to the cursory observer, that the police do not enforce all the laws in low-income neighborhoods that they would in middle class areas. One reason is the sheer crush of business which makes it difficult to police all but major infractions. In the Bronx, Manhattan and Brooklyn, policemen said that pressures of their job force them to overlook numbers running, street gambling, pot smoking, small narcotics traffic, petty shop lifting. "Drug addicts are like roaches," said one Lower East Side police officer in an attitude resigned to defeat or only temporary victo-

ry, one well understood by most New Yorkers. In every precinct and neighborhood the police and residents alike can tick
off the main drug-selling blocks. The police argue that they
have no men to go after narcotics in a significant way. Community residents are convinced that lack of enforcement
means the police are on the take.

In Bushwick we were in a patrol car as it turned the corner
near Broadway and suddenly came on a group of twelve men
bent over the curb in a sidewalk dice game. Far from running
away or even trying to hide what they were doing, the men
simply stared as the patrol car slipped by. The policeman driving smiled weakly and gave them a little wave. "We just don't
have enough time to bother with things like that," he said. "If
we arrested them, we'd have to get men out here to guard
them, do all the paper work. There's just no time."

On the Lower East Side, Puerto Rican social clubs are
technically in violation of the law when they sell beer to non-
members, as they often do. Yet the police have other things to
do with their day besides make them obey the law. "If that's
all it takes to make them happy, hey, who cares?" said the
captain of one precinct. "You've seen the way these people
have to live around here!"

The main thoroughfares of Harlem are lined with flea markets dealing in stolen goods, petty fences stop people on the
street to offer record albums, watches, pocket calculators,
jewelry. One jeweler on 125th Street believes his store was
spared the night of the looting because the local class of
thieves needs him as its official appraiser. "All day long," he
said, "guys are coming in here with watches and stuff. 'Hey,
Mike, how much is this worth? How much can I sell this
for?' "

Such an enforcement pattern—or, rather, the lack of
one—serves a purpose in that it allows the police to keep the
community under control with a minimal expenditure of manpower and resources. Many policemen, however, see the lack
of law enforcement not as a logistical compromise but as
something that reflects what the community at large *wants*

from its constabulary. "Let's face it," said Sergeant Freud of the 24th Precinct on the Upper West Side of Manhattan. "People in these communities tolerate things that other places wouldn't tolerate. The community gets the kind of policing it deserves."[1]

The feeling among many of the police that residents of poor communities actually want them to overlook certain kinds of criminal conduct may have explained the impression among witnesses to the looting that some policemen did not do all they could to stop the stealing. "They could have done more than they did," said youth worker Aubrey Edmonds. "It was like they wanted to see you fuck up what you had, so they let you go ahead and do it."

"I felt really bad for the city that night," said one Puerto Rican anticrime patrolman in the West Bronx. "I was standing there watching the stealing and it was eating the heart out of me. The people were so stupid—they didn't see they were only hurting themselves. But the majority of the police officers, I would say, were laughing at it. Some of them were taking advantage of the overtime, seeing how much time they could get, seeing what they could get out of the night."

Whatever the reason for selective law enforcement in ghetto areas, it clearly creates the strong impression, especially among the young, that the law is not exactly inviolate and that some criminal activity is acceptable behavior. The effect of this empirical lesson was dramatically brought home to the police the night of the blackout. Many patrolmen spoke with great amazement of how surprised looters seemed when they were actually arrested. "They couldn't understand why we were arresting them," said Patrolman Gary Parlefsky of the 30th Precinct in West Harlem.

"You'd grab a kid in a store," added another patrolman from the 83rd Precinct in Bushwick, "and they'd look at you as if they weren't doing anything! As if you had no right to stop them!"

In the end, enforcing the law, keeping impoverished minority neighborhoods cool and instilling respect for the police might indeed all be contradictory aims. It is hardly surprising that patrolmen placed under such pressure increasingly become victims of cynicism, bitterness and demoralization.

"I've just about had it," said a patrolman who works on a plainclothes anticrime patrol in the 44th Precinct in Highbridge. "When I became a police officer I thought my job was to help the community, I really mean that," says the beleaguered officer, who averages forty-five felony arrests a year, about triple the normal rate for a patrolman in uniform.

But all I deal with are criminals. Here the people don't like police officers because all we do is arrest their brothers and fathers. I'm tired of getting dirty looks from them. You get a call and catch a burglar in their apartment, and even then they say you're doing them an injustice. In the blackout, you go and try to grab a guy with a TV set, and you get bottles thrown at you. Everytime you go on the block, you get called a motherfucker. I feel sometimes like getting out of the car and strangling them.

His own car in the precinct parking lot was vandalized recently by someone who inscribed a line with a can opener along the body. Another time his windshield was broken, and in a third instance, he discovered the lug nuts on his wheel had been taken off and the hub cap replaced. Fortunately the wheel fell off before he drove out of the parking lot, he said. Another policeman's car was set afire.

"All the commotion," he said. "I'm seeing a doctor because I've started having stomach troubles. I'd like a light-duty precinct where maybe the people would have a little respect for the police."

Indeed, the failure of the police to cope with the blackout looting was only an exaggerated example of their inability to cope with ghetto crime in general at all times. In a 1970 study for the Rand Institute, Peter Greenwood found in an analysis of the NYPD's arrest rate that ". . . only 9 robberies out of 100 result in an arrest at the scene; the probability of such arrests for burglary and grand larceny is only .04. Not only do most criminals escape from the locus of the crime unscathed, but the probability of follow-up investigations leading to arrest are quite small: .06 for robbery and .02 for burglary and grand larceny."[2]

This is true not only for New York. In his survey of law enforcement in St. Louis and other cities, James P. Levine concludes: ". . . the criminal has the odds in his favor and can operate with relative impunity; the old slogan, 'crime does not pay' is wrong; the risks are surely much lower than those entailed in most legitimate business pursuits."[3]

vii

PROFILE OF THE ARRESTED LOOTERS: INCOME AND UNEMPLOYMENT

In Chapter II we examined the way in which the looting population shifted during the course of the blackout. Therefore it is reasonable to conclude that the profiles of the arrestees are not strongly representative of all the looters. But the fact that original analyses of arrestees by public officials and the press represented the looters as a relatively well-off group, led many people to believe that poverty had little or nothing to do with the disturbances. In the *New York Times/* CBS poll, only 39 percent of those New Yorkers interviewed agreed with the statement that the looters were "out of work and frustrated."[1] Thus whether or not the looters were really poor becomes one of the most important considerations in making judgments about what happened during the blackout. It also forms an important basis on which we can judge whether or not the looters did, in fact, have a "message." That is why in this chapter we have devoted so much space to reviewing what was said about the looters and where it was said, before analyzing the data.

By the time the lights returned in all the boroughs, 3,076 people had been arrested and charged with a variety of offenses including assault, criminal trespass, and burglary in the first, second and third degree. There were also charges for possession of a weapon (leveled at merchants as well as at looters), criminal mischief, grand larceny, robbery, possession of stolen property, arson, and inciting to riot. Both the State of New York Division of Criminal Justice Services and the New York City Criminal Justice Agency conducted extensive analyses on the individuals arrested. The following discussion draws heavily on these sources.

The largest number of arrests, 1,088, occurred in Brooklyn, while 961 were arrested in the Bronx, 836 in Manhattan, 191 in Queens and 30 in Staten Island. Of those arrested, only 6.7 percent were women; nearly 1,600, or more than half, of the entire group fell between the ages of 16 and 25. Juveniles accounted for 173 of the arrestees; the youngest were two 11-year-olds. Conversely 232, or 8 percent of the arrestees, were over the age of 40. Blacks comprised 65.3 percent of the arrestees; 30.3 percent were Hispanic and 4 percent were white. According to the State Division of Criminal Justice study, 56.1 percent of the arrestees had prior arrest records, a more accurate appraisal of arrest history than the 64.4 percent figures given by the New York City Criminal Justice Agency, since subsequent court dispositions favorable to the defendant were excluded.

The Gold Report

Nearly a month after the blackout, Brooklyn District Attorney Eugene Gold released an analysis of 176 indicted looters at a press conference widely covered by local news media.

Reporting on the August 9 conference the *New York Times* wrote:

Of the 176 persons indicted on looting charges after last month's blackout, almost half had full-time jobs and less than 10% were on welfare. . . .

According to Gold's statistics, 48% were employed with average incomes of $135.50 a week or about $7,050 a year reported. Eleven percent were listed as students and 41% as unemployed.

He said that 8.5% of the 176 persons indicted reported that they were on welfare. . . .

Gold was reported as concluding that these statistics "belied statements made earlier by President Carter and others that the looting had been committed by hungry people."[2]

The *Daily News* dropped the *Times*'s "almost" and said simply that "half of those arrested in Brooklyn had fulltime jobs."[3] They also cited an additional figure attributed to Gold: that "57 percent were single making an average annual salary of $7,050." Like the *Times*, the *News* quoted Gold as saying that "these figures dispute a great deal of what has been said about the looters."

Examining Gold's statistical findings, it seems that both newspapers made serious errors in reporting. The district attorney provided reporters with a list containing the names, addresses, occupations and income of the looters whose indictments he was announcing. Of the 176 individuals listed, only 66, or 37.5 percent, were listed as having any form of employment. The remaining 110 indicted looters were listed as either unemployed (58, or 33 percent), occupation unknown (36, or 20.5 percent), or students (16, or 9 percent).

Furthermore, our count indicates that 19 of the 66 listed as employed were recorded by Gold as earning less than $110 a week. The average salary of these 19 was approximately $75 a week. This group of marginally employed individuals brings the number of "fully employed" indicted looters to 47, or less than 27 percent. Yet the newspapers had concluded that half, or "almost half," of the looters had fulltime jobs.

Income figures were also reported incorrectly. Gold's release said that the average income of "those who reported their income" was $135.50 a week, or approximately "$7,050 a year." Income data was listed by Gold for only 46 individuals, or 26 percent of the 176 indicted looters. Yet the *News* reported that "57 percent were single, making an average annual salary of $7,050 a year." The *Times* said "48 percent were employed with average incomes of . . . about $7,050 a year."

In addition, Gold's original data on income was inaccurately tabulated. Our count of the 46 weekly salaries listed by Gold comes to an average of $126.50 a week, or $6,570 a year. It is important to note that those income figures were taken from about 4 percent of the total arrested looter population in Brooklyn and were not a scientific sampling.

One reason the newspapers erred in reporting this data was the confusing way in which Gold summarized it on a separate table attached to his press release. The table separated those whose employment status was listed as "unknown," and stated that 48 percent of the remaining 140 indicted looters were employed. The newspapers then took the 48 percent figure and applied it to the total number of 176 indicted looters. This initial mistake was compounded when the press added the income data atop the spurious foundation of the miscalculated employment data. When a study deals with so small a sample of a total population, a single mistake like this can skew the entire result.

The 20.5 percent of Gold's indicted looters whose employment status was "unknown" contrasts sharply with the 6 percent figure of "unknowns" in the normal Brooklyn arrest population. Robert Keating, Gold's chief assistant, readily concedes that most of the "unknowns" on Gold's list were most probably "unemployed," since virtually all of those with employment would have listed it to enhance their chances for bail.

The welfare status of the arrested looters was also a source of confusion. Gold told the press that 8.5 percent of the indicted defendants were on welfare, as compared to the

15.7 percent of normal arrestees who are on welfare. But this difference is not an indication that indicted looters were any better off than normal arrestees economically, as was widely interpreted. Only 6 (or 3 percent) of the indicted looters on Gold's list were women, as opposed to 16 percent of the normal defendant population. Since most indicted looters were single men in their twenties who account for an extremely low portion of the welfare population, it is not surprising that the incidence of welfare is low. Indeed, it would be surprising if it were high.

The problems of the Gold study, however, go beyond its presentation and the press reporting. The source of Gold's data, according to Keating, were interviews with defendants conducted by the Pre-Trial Services Agency, a creation of the Vera Institute of Justice.

At the time, PTSA was a private agency funded through the city's Criminal Justice Coordinating Council by city and federal funds. Its functions included interviewing defendants after arrest and before arraignment to make release recommendations to the court, and notifying released defendants of their court-related obligations.

PTSA interviewed these defendants on July 13, 14, 15 and 16 while they awaited Criminal Court arraignment in Brooklyn, Manhattan and the Bronx. The interviews were conducted in the crowded, raucous conditions of the detention pens. In August 1977, shortly after the completion of these interviews, PTSA's functions were assumed by another agency, the NYC Criminal Justice Agency (CJA). CJA described the PTSA interviews of blackout defendants as follows:

The primary purpose is to provide the courts with an assessment of the risk of flight . . . Defendants found to possess strong community ties as evidenced by the length of residence in the community, the type of family structure and the length of employment are recommended by PTSA as good risks for release without bond. Because these recommendations are based on an analysis of the strength of the community ties of each defendant, these interviews also serve to provide a demographic profile on the blackout defendants.[4]

Our own check of a random selection of those listed by PTSA as employed suggests that the agency tended to put their circumstances in the best possible light. For example, Christopher Perkins listed by Gold and PTSA as a $135-a-week printer, works at a company in a training position making industrial tags. He said to us that he told the PTSA interviewer that he makes $88 a week. Christopher was then asked how much he could make with overtime, and he said that he might make as much as $135. He said he reiterated the fact that he only makes $88 and that, as a trainee, he has never worked overtime.

Steven Jones, listed by Gold and PTSA as a bedspring maker earning $150 a week, had a similar experience. Steven was not at home when we visited him, but his mother told us that he only makes $150 a week if he works overtime. She showed us two pay slips indicating that in one recent week he made $149; but in another, he earned $66. The first week's high salary was due to overtime. Moreover Steven is now unemployed. The bedspring company he works for operates on a seasonal schedule, and Steven is jobless at least three months a year. When working, Steven's average pay—says his mother—is about $100 a week. Steven is a marginally employed man whose job was converted by PTSA into a full-time, well-paid position so he would get a better deal from the courts.

Otis Tibbs is listed by Gold as a "manager" earning $200 a week. Otis says that this listing by PTSA caused him great difficulty in obtaining Legal Aid representation as an indigent person. When he was interviewed by PTSA, Otis says he told them that he earned approximately $200 a week, but that his expenses were over $100 a week. Therefore his actual earnings were less than $100 a week. Otis is not a manager; he is a gypsy cab driver and must pay for his car and gas. "I explained all of that at the time, but I guess they didn't understand," he said.

Mitchell Williams, listed as a part-time contractor earning $175 a week, is actually a laborer. His weekly salary is correct but he said he is frequently laid off for long periods of time.

Our check also revealed that five of the twelve checked at random did not live where they were listed by Gold. In two instances, the building superintendent said they had lived there, but had moved more than a year before the blackout. In a sixth case, we attempted to find the man at a boutique listed on his PTSA form as employer. The store had been out of business for months.

In only two of the twelve cases checked by us at the homes or businesses of suspects were we able to confirm the income-employment data of Gold and PTSA. This is not to say that we believe the suspects were telling us the truth and that either PTSA misrepresented their statement or that the defendants lied to PTSA. What it means is that the poor are used to wearing a thousand faces when they confront official questions. The same defendant may describe himself as employed when attempting to qualify for release without bail and as unemployed when seeking assistance from Legal Aid. Indeed it is clear that this is precisely what occurred on a massive scale. A *Times* story two weeks after the blackout reported that the Legal Aid Society, by its own estimate, represented 70 to 75 percent of the blackout defendants.[5] This estimate was of representation at *arraignment,* which was at precisely the same time that PTSA was interviewing defendants and gathering the data that profiled the average defendant as employed and well-heeled. The Legal Aid caseload of blackout defendants has remained at roughly the same percentage throughout the judicial process.

The point is that any data which depends solely on the unverified assertion of a defendant seeking release, is at best uncertain. When the purpose of the question changes, so might the thrust of the answer.

We conducted two other tests of the Gold-PTSA data. Gold's category of 46 indicted looters with stated incomes included several individuals whose employers were listed by Gold. We checked 12 of them, and half of the employers said the individuals were not employed by them. In two instances the individuals had been briefly employed by these companies, but had not worked there for more than a year prior to their blackout arrest.

We also examined indictment files maintained in Brooklyn Supreme Court on 20 of the indicted looters listed by Gold. Each folder contains an arrest record filled out by the arresting officer, who asks the defendant if he or she is employed and then records the answer. The form is apparently not included in the file maintained by the district attorney, although the court file is certainly available to the DA's office. In 4 of the 20 cases checked, Gold and PTSA had listed as employed, individuals who were recorded by the arresting officer as unemployed. In 2 other instances, employment status was listed by Gold as "unknown," but as "unemployed" on the arrest records.

We were restricted to examining the court files of finished cases, but this random check suggests that defendants changed the description of their employment status depending upon who was asking the question. It also suggests that defendants were more willing to describe themselves as employed to PTSA. Gold's chief assistant, Keating, told us that "as soon as he knows who he's talking to," a criminal defendant "will tend to stretch the truth." He conceded that his office "could not do a demographic report from the data we had."

* * *

The only other data on employment among Brooklyn arrestees came from interview sheets at the 79th Precinct which shares patrol of Bedford-Stuyvesant with the 81st and 77th. Looking at information provided by the 117 persons arrested by the 79th that night suggests that only a few of them participate in the nation's economy.

Of the 117 arrestees, 9 were students, 2 were storeowners arrested on gun charges, 1 was a housewife and 1 a retiree. Of the remaining 104 arrestees, 69, or 66 percent, told police they were unemployed. Of the 35 who said they had some kind of job, many were only marginally employed. Ten gave answers indicating they were casual laborers; 7 worked in publicly funded manpower projects, including one for the Wildcat Service Corporation and two for the Restoration Corporation. Four listed their work simply as "carpenter," or "painter," and 14 said they had jobs in restaurants, stores and the like.

* * *

In addition to characterizing the looters as not particularly poor, District Attorney Gold also offered a profile of those who were looted. The *Daily News* quoted him as stating: "The targets of looters were 39 furniture stores, 20 drugstores, 18 appliance stores and 17 jewelry stores. Two supermarkets, 6 grocery stores and 4 butcher shops also were looted." This data was cited by Gold as further refutation of the contention "that the majority of the looters were jobless and needed food for their families."[6]

Yet according to the City Planning Commission, the number of Brooklyn groceries, supermarkets and meat and fish markets looted or damaged was not the 12 totaled by Gold but 89, many of which consisted of cleaned-out large supermarkets. This count coincides with the citywide numbers which list clothing and food stores as the most often looted businesses that night.

Gold's figures were arrived at by adding up the stores looted by the individuals he was indicting. Since felony indictments were most often handed down in cases involving the looting of valuable property, rather than groceries, the list of stores was skewed toward furniture, jewelry and appliance stores. The *Daily News* version of the Gold press conference was headlined: "Study of Looters Disputes Claims of Hunger," or, in a later edition, "Finds Looters Not Hungry."[7]

For his part, Gold used his interpretation of the data to justify the prosecutorial posture he simultaneously announced: "None of these people are going to get off by pleading to a misdemeanor. They will have to go to trial unless they are willing to plea bargain to a felony."

The Scoppetta Report

Five days after Gold released his report, Deputy Mayor for Criminal Justice Nicholas Scoppetta released a citywide study of 2,707 adult, blackout-related defendants. The *Times* reported that Scoppetta's findings confirmed the earlier study conducted by Gold.[8]

In a front-page story on the Scoppetta data, the *Times* wrote:

The first comprehensive survey of suspects seized citywide . . . shows that 45% of the adults arrested had jobs—an employment rate half again as high as the rate among those normally arrested for crimes in New York City. . . .

These and other findings, criminal justice experts said, could help produce important new insights into the nature of civil disorders . . . the survey might show that there was less of a connection than many analysts had contended between the jobless rate in impoverished neighborhoods and the incidence of disorders such as those last month.

The *Daily News* reported:

Suspects arrested during the blackout crime wave were—on the average—not poor, nonwhite youths with fairly stable roots in their communities. . . .

[The report's] figures raise a challenge to preconceptions about the crime wave and set forth a new, *closely documented* set of statistics about the extent of the looting.[9] (emphasis added)

A look at Scoppetta's data suggests that it was about as "closely documented" and "comprehensive" as that released by Gold's office. Like Gold's, Scoppetta's data is entirely based on PTSA interviews. Unlike Gold, however, Scoppetta revealed the source of the data and cautioned against making sweeping conclusions. The back tables of his report even demonstrated how unreliable the data was. The table breaks the 2,707 arrestees in his study into two categories: Those whose cases PTSA reviewed for bail recommendations (1,201) and those it did not review (1,506). Of the 1,201 cases reviewed citywide, PTSA only verified the employment status of 79, or 6 percent. It did not verify the employment status of any of the 1,506 cases it failed to review for bail. This means that PTSA actually verified the income and employment data of *only 3 percent* of the defendants in the city.

The Scoppetta report was widely interpreted as a verification of the early study released by Gold's office. But instead of confirming Gold's statistics, it really demonstrated how unreliable they were. Gold, it turns out, was using the most unverified figures in the city: Only 2 percent of Brooklyn's 732 defendants reviewed by PTSA and only 1 percent of the total of 1,051 defendants were verified. The Scoppetta table contrasts this 2 percent figure with the 46.8 percent verification rate for all defendants arraigned in Brooklyn during normal operating procedure (the period used for comparison was May 30 to June 26, 1977). The normal citywide rate of verification, using the same period, is 38.5 percent.

PTSA officials have confirmed that the agency "suspended" verification efforts during the blackout emergency. A PTSA official told us that while he has no documentation, he believes unverified data is roughly as accurate as verified data, but he said the agency seeks to verify anyway because without verification, judges refuse to accept PTSA recommendations.

There were other significant problems with Scoppetta's data. Like Gold's listing of indicted looters, there was a disproportionate number of arrestees whose employment status was "Unknown." Some 21 percent of Gold's sample were listed as unknown, and 25 percent of Scoppetta's 2,707 total were listed as "missing" on the employment status table. This contrasts with a 5 percent missing or unknown rate for a comparison group of citywide defendants randomly selected between June 6 and June 12, 1977, and reported as part of Scoppetta's employment table. This difference in the "unknown" category may be the only explanation for the claimed difference in employment patterns cited by Scoppetta and Gold. This is especially true in view of Keating's conclusion that most of those listed as unknown are probably unemployed.

The final arguments against the figures were made by Scoppetta when he released them. The numbers purport to compare the employment, income, and so on, of blackout defendants against all those arrested—regardless of charge—during another time frame. As the report warns, this is statistically unsound since it compares defendants accused of dissimilar crimes. The statistics do not, for example, compare looters with those accused of burglary or crimes against property in ordinary times. They compare looters with all defendants.

Finally there is a certain irony in the Scoppetta-Gold data and the use to which it was put by the press and the public as a means of characterizing the looting defendants. The original PTSA interviews were made in extraordinary circumstances. By all accounts, judges were setting bail in excess—in some instances, as we will detail, far in excess—of ordinary amounts. The mood in the courtrooms was hardened and angry. Information about the judicial temperament was filtering back into the detention pens. Defendants were under pressure. Under these circumstances, it is not unreasonable to assume that PTSA interviewers, who were used to a more gentle judicial approach, may have reacted to the new temperament. The pressure from the courtroom was in one direction, and the skewing of income-employment-roots data to place defendants in the best light was a response to it. The paradox is that PTSA's advocacy profiles of individuals were used to support conclusions that the looters were not poor at all, but merely greedy criminals.

These portrayals, in turn, contributed further to the long-term hardening of the judicial treatment of the arrested looters, which we shall examine in the next chapter.

THE CRIMINAL JUSTICE SYSTEM

Detention

Government studies and news reports agree that arrested looters saw a harder side of the law than that encountered by average arrestees. *Newsweek* magazine offered the most detailed journalistic description:

At the height of the city's worst heat wave in ten years, prisoners were detained incommunicado in nightmarish quarters. The detention pens where prisoners stay until their arraignments are cramped and short on sanitary facilities. There are no kitchens, and since prisoners rarely spend even one night, bedding is almost unheard of.

Outside the Brooklyn Court Detention Facility, the temperature was nearly 100 degrees. Inside it was more like 120. Two dozen men were jammed for five days in an 8-by-12 cell that usually holds four or five for a matter of hours. The fetid smell of urine and sweat hung in the air.[1]

The New York State Select Committee on Criminal Justice Emergency Preparedness (CJEP), a group assigned by Governor Carey to review the response of the criminal justice system, issued a similar description:

Many defendants were jammed into pre-arraignment facilities not designed for long-term use, but for stays of only a few hours. Court detention pens were cramped and unbearably hot. No recreational facilities were available, and since defendants rarely stay overnight there was insufficient bedding. Telephone service for calls to families was unavailable in sufficient degree. Food service was inadequate. Sanitary facilities and medical attention (particularly for drug addicts) were not adequate for the number of people detained. The Commissioner of the NYC Department of Correction acknowledged that the court pens did not meet minimum standards for correctional institutions and admitted that too many people were there too long. He described conditions in the Brooklyn pens as "the worst I've ever seen."

"The difficult circumstances under which criminal justice personnel were compelled to operate do not excuse the inhumane conditions into which detainees were thrown.[2]

Sixty-two percent of the arrestees, by city figures, waited in these pens for three or more days before they were arraigned.[3] Normally, according to the CJEP, a burglary defendant is arraigned within fourteen hours of arrest. The longest waits were in the boroughs where the worst conditions prevailed. For example, in Brooklyn, 239 arrestees were arraigned on July 19, six days after most of them were arrested. Twelve of these individuals had been arrested seven days prior to arraignment. In fact more arrestees were arraigned on July 19 in Brooklyn than on any previous day. This contrasts sharply with Manhattan, where only one arraignment was delayed until July 19. In Manhattan 93 percent of the arrestees were arraigned by the end of the day on July 17. In Brooklyn barely half were arraigned by July 17. In Manhattan more than half of the defendants were arraigned by July 15, the day after the looting. Only 20 percent of Brooklyn's defendants were arraigned by July 15.[4] These disparities cannot be attributed to a large difference in the number of arrested looters, since there were close to 1,000 in each borough.

In the Bronx 30 percent of the 943 arrestees were arraigned by the end of July 15, somewhere between Brooklyn's 20 percent and Manhattan's 50 percent. In Queens 90 percent of the looters were arraigned by July 15, but there were only 191 arraignments throughout the period.

Most observers have pinned much of the responsibility for these delays on the police and prosecutors. The state's Select Committee reported:

As officers returned from the street with their prisoners, continued and widespread looting dictated that they return to the streets. Their redeployment separated the officers from their prisoners and resulted in the postponement of routine arrest processing paperwork. . . .

Some officers were reassigned to other areas of the city, resulting in subsequent difficulty in locating and notifying them for arraignment. Numerous instances occurred in which a defendant was brought to court but an arresting officer was unavailable to testify. . . .

In many instances, when officers were returned to the streets, other officers were assigned to take charge of their prisoners for arraignment processing. Inadequate paperwork at the initial processing stage left escorting officers with insufficient knowledge of the facts . . . ADA's [assistant district attorneys] were unable to complete the complaint.[5]

Other serious arraignment delays were caused by the interruption of "the vital flow of fingerprints to and from Albany" and problems in the custody and movement of prisoners.

In any case, what seems clear is that the delay in arraignment cannot be attributed to the courts: the New York State Office of Court Administration issued a report indicating that an emergency doubling of the number of arraignment parts in Criminal Courts throughout the city enabled the courts to handle twice the number of defendants as were actually processed. For example, in Brooklyn on July 15, the number of arraignment parts was doubled, meaning that 600 arrestees could have been arraigned. Only 70 actually were. On no day except July 19 did Brooklyn arraign even half of the number of defendants that the courts were prepared for. Courts were kept open around the clock in Brooklyn, yet for long periods of time no arraignments occurred.

The state's Office of Court Administration concluded: "During these five days, the arraignment parts were often idle for lack of business. On Sunday, July 17, the daytime arraignment parts in the Bronx had no defendants to arraign until 3:30 P.M. On Tuesday, July 19, in the Bronx, only four cases were furnished the courts for arraignment up to 3:00 P.M., although three arraignment parts had been awaiting cases since 9:30 A.M."[6]

These facts forced the Select Committee to conclude that the court process was the single aspect of the justice system "which experienced the least difficulty in maintaining operations."[7] State Administrative Judge Richard J. Bartlett and City Administrative Judge David Ross stated that blackout defendants were promptly arraigned "within an hour" of the filing of the charges. The problem, then, was getting the police and the prosecutors to file the charges.

The reasons why Manhattan processed cases more rapidly than the Bronx or Brooklyn are suggested by a couple of side comments in the Select Committee Report:

In Manhattan, judges, prosecutors, and defense attorneys cooperated to permit initial arraignment without criminal history records, subject to bail re-evaluation. This process alleviated the burden of police custody by transferring prisoners from overcrowded pre-arraignment facilities to Department of Correction facilities. . . .

"In some precincts, instant pictures were taken of prisoners and arresting officers immediately following arrest, greatly facilitating subsequent identification and arrest processing. This procedure was not uniformly followed throughout the city.[8]

Our own findings, after visits with more than a dozen precincts, indicate that Manhattan precincts adopted these photo identification procedures to a much greater degree than did those in the Bronx and Brooklyn.

The absence of these arrest identification procedures and, more particularly, of an agreement to waive the criminal record requirement, contributed to the arraignment delays in Brooklyn and the Bronx. What may have also contributed was a tendency, in the Bronx particularly, to minimize weekend arraignments. The State's Office of Court Administration states that only 69 cases were docketed for arraignment on Saturday, July 17, as compared to 345 that Monday. The arraignment parts open on Saturday were capable of handling 200 cases.

Similarly on Sunday, July 17, the state office indicates that, in the Bronx, no defendants were ready for arraignment until 3:30 P.M. Between that time and the end of the day, 152 looting defendants were arraigned. These numbers suggest a weekend hiatus in the Bronx: for a day and a half the arraignment process ground to a virtual halt, while 540 Bronx arrestees awaiting arraignment remained cramped in detention pens.

Though not as dramatic, the numbers in Brooklyn also suggest a lower level of activity during the post-blackout weekend. According to state court figures, 696 total cases were docketed for arraignment in Brooklyn on Monday and Tuesday, July 18 and 19. But only 389 cases were docketed for arraignment on the weekend of July 16–17. Approximately 500 blackout defendants awaiting arraignment spent that weekend in detention facilities.

On the other hand, courts in Manhattan demonstrated a sense of urgency about processing the arrestees. Arraignment parts in Manhattan were available to process 400 cases on Saturday, July 16, and 333 were docketed for arraignment. The bulk of blackout arraignments in Manhattan was completed by the end of the day on Saturday, so that the total number of cases docketed for Sunday arraignment dropped to 176. Only 49 blackout defendants were detained in Manhattan for arraignment on Monday and Tuesday.

Arraignment

Getting to arraignment was but a small part of the problem. Once arraigned, the accused looter became a special case. The New York City Criminal Justice Agency examined the handling of 2,677 arraignments of blackout-related defendants and compared the outcomes with a control group of all defendants (1,841) arraigned between July 4 and July 10, 1977.[9]

Since this comparison group involves all defendants for a particular period, regardless of the crime committed, it contains certain flaws. The comparison group includes arrests for violent and other crimes more serious than third degree burglary (the typical looting indictment), so that the differences in treatment on remands and releases might be greater were the comparison group to include only other burglary defendants.

What is evident in these numbers—though not commented on by the agency—is that 70 percent of the normal arrest groups walk in and out of court: either their case is dismissed or they are released on their own recognizance. Only 27 percent of the blackout-related defendants were freed. You were almost three times as likely to face bail or be jailed if arrested as a looter than if you had been an average defendant a week earlier. You were also eight times as likely to be remanded to jail if you were a blackout defendant (16 percent of the total defendants) than if you had been arrested for any crime the week before (2 percent of the total defendants). You were more than twice as likely to be held on bail if you were a blackout defendant (57 percent of all blackout defendants vs. 27 percent of the total comparison group).

The group of 428 blackout defendants remanded to jail on their first court appearance included 62 whose cases were later dismissed and 93 who were subsequently released on their own recognizance. In 81 cases no change was made in their status in subsequent court appearances, and in 192 cases bail was eventually set.

One of the reasons why more blackout-related defendants were remanded to jail than the comparison group was that in cases in which no criminal record information could be located, defendants were remanded until this information could be obtained. This might explain remands if they were concentrated in Manhattan, where a specific agreement was reached between Legal Aid and the District Attorney which permitted arraignment without access to prior record. But Manhattan had fewer remands than Brooklyn or the Bronx, slightly more than a quarter of the total number. And though Manhattan remands were made without benefit of prior record information, fewer than 6 percent of the 116 Manhattan remands were dismissed at the first court appearance, while much higher percentages were dismissed in the Bronx and Brooklyn.

The high rate of remands in all these boroughs, therefore, cannot be substantially explained by the absence of criminal record information. In subsequent court appearances the status of remanded defendants was changed in 80 percent of the cases. Almost half of those whose status changed, were released.

There is no comprehensive statistical analysis of the bails set on blackout-related defendants. But some of the news reporting hints at a tendency toward harshness on bail set for blackout defendants. *Newsweek* reported:

"Many judges admitted setting stiff bails—some as high as $5,000—but denied that the sums were excessive. 'Because this happened in an emergency, it was more than just burglary,' said Judge A. Fredrick Meyerson, who was working double shifts in Brooklyn Criminal Court. 'These defendants were there to loot stores.'"[10]

According to a survey in the *New York Post*, bail in the Bronx ranged from $500 to $1,500, and in Queens, from $500 to $3,000.[11] Robert Spadaro, an assistant district attorney in Brooklyn, told us that he usually asked for and got $5,000 to $10,000 bail on the "bad guys" (who had prior criminal records) and $2,500 on the "good guys."

"We asked for very high bail in every case and we were

able to get it almost every time," Spadaro said. "Sometimes you ask for a dollar and get a dime [in bail], but in these looting cases we would ask for a dollar and the judge would set bail at ten."

Judges we talked to agreed that when it came to bail, looting defendants were indeed special cases. "Because it was an emergency situation which bordered on anarchy, bail was set higher than usual," said Judge Meyerson. "These defendants had to learn that the City of New York and the criminal justice system would not tolerate this kind of conduct."

Another Brooklyn judge told us: "I've lived in this borough all my life and I've seen it at its worst, and now getting better. I did think that here we had something very wrong and I know that I was thinking about what the good people had a right to expect as I set bail."

For defendants who have money or a good credit rating, bail is simply an amount of cash held by the court to help insure their appearance for trial. In the meantime, they are free to assist in the preparation of their defense. For the poor, as has been frequently noted, bail often amounts to a jail sentence itself—sometimes even when it is set at what appears to most people as a very low figure. In *Police, Criminal Justice and the Community*, criminologists Alan Bent and Ralph Rossum point out that "when bail is set at more than $500 it often becomes more than most defendants can afford."[12] A recent New York City study found that 25 percent of all defendants cannot make bail at $500, 45 percent fail at $1,500 and 63 percent, at $2,500.[13] A Legal Aid lawyer handling blackout cases told us: "For our clients, to have a judge set $250 or $500 cash bail is like a million dollars. There's simply no way in the world that they're going to make it."

Neither were judges following their normal tendency to release defendants who could demonstrate that they had roots in the community. Using their own PTSA data on community ties, the Criminal Justice Agency noted: "To the extent that the strength of community ties reflects a good risk for release on recognizance, the courts did not release these defendants

at a rate consistent with pre-existing patterns. Both disposition and ROR rates of arraignment for the blackout defendants were unusually low."[14]

According to several Legal Aid attorneys, a final consequence of blackout bail practices was that a defendant who
was unable to meet an initial high bail was more likely to be indicted on felony charges than one who could meet bail and get
off the court's docket for a few weeks. Under state law, defendants who cannot meet bail must be given a hearing within
seventy-two hours of their arraignment. This brought the
poorest looters back into the courtroom at the height of public
indignation against them. In many instances that meant their
cases would immediately be referred to a grand jury for indictment. On the other hand, those alleged looters who were
able to meet bail after it was first set were given a later court
date, often long after the public furor had died down. Legal
Aid attorney Noah Hauft told us: "Someone charged with
burglary was indicted right away if he couldn't make bail,
while someone charged with exactly the same thing who could
make bail was able to come back later, when things had
cooled down, and get off with as little as a violation or a misdemeanor."

Sentencing

The arraignment delays, the poor detention conditions, the
high rate of remands to jail and the insistence on bail were in
part a reflection of the mood in the community toward the
looting and in part the product of an overloaded justice system. Taken together, however, they all seem to fall into the
punitive pattern of the official response to the blackout arrests. Marshall Sohne, another Legal Aid attorney, called
them "sentencing devices" and said: "In one conference at
the bench we told the judge that bail was tremendously high

and he said, 'You know these guys [the accused looters] won't be punished later, so we're gonna get them now.' '' *Newsweek* found a similar sentiment among the judges. After describing the conditions blackout defendants suffered, *Newsweek* said:

"Some city judges even see a possible bright spot in all of this. Many of the people who endured the ordeal in the detention cells, they suggest, may take extra care to make sure they never have to come back."[15]

Of less concern in the process was the presumption of innocence. Although 1,129 cases had yet to be decided as of October 12, 1977, the date of the first comprehensive survey of disposition, the results up until that date are instructive. Some 279 of the looting cases had been dismissed by October 12; many were dismissed at arraignment or at a second hearing. Another 79 were "adjourned in contemplation of dismissal."[1] Two of the four that went to trial resulted in acquittal. Eighteen percent of the cases decided by October 12 had resulted in dismissal or acquittal. Another 93 defendants were reclassified as juveniles and sent to family court or treated as youthful offenders, raising to 453 (almost 22 percent) the number of defendants who had been subjected to the same conditions as those who had pled guilty.

In all, 1,220 blackout defendants had pled guilty by October 12. Of these, 79 percent were sentenced but not returned to jail. Their dispositions, in order of the frequency of occurrence were: time served (427), conditional discharge (226), fine plus time served (190), probation (69), fine (38), and unconditional discharge (8). These figures dramatize the system's dependence for punishment on factors other than sentencing; namely bail, remands, detention and arraignment delays.

Of the 262 defendants who received additional jail terms, about half were sentenced to 30 days. Only 14 got as much as a year.

These figures do not include the dispositions of many cases that resulted in indictments. Plea bargaining and trials continued into the spring, with the defendant's fate depending in large part on which borough he or she happened to get arrested in. Making good on his original prosecutorial pledge, Brooklyn's District Attorney Gold wound up indicting 300 of his blackout defendants—roughly 30 percent of the total—far more than in any other borough and far more than the normal percentage of indictments for felony arrests.

In the Bronx, District Attorney Mario Merola differed with Gold on the kind of people who were arrested that night. "The fact is that the majority of the people arrested were scavengers," he told the *New York Post* two weeks after the blackout. [17] "The really bad guys who tore down the gates and ripped off the expensive stuff were gone when the police got there." Not surprisingly, he also dealt differently with the defendants when it came to prosecution: only 10 percent of the approximately 900 arrestees in the Bronx were indicted.

A report issued on July 12, 1978 by Richard J. Bartlett, Chief Administrative Judge of the New York State courts, and by Frank J. Rogers, Commissioner of the New York State Division of Criminal Justice Services, provides the most recent account of blackout cases. It further confirms what the earlier report suggested: That the looting defendants were treated unusually harsh by the judicial system. Judging solely from the sentences meted out at trial, it would seem that looters got off comparatively light. But these sentences did not take into account the fact that a large percentage of the arrestees had already received punishment before trial, in the form of excessive bail and long detention.

At the time of their report, less than 8 percent of the cases were still pending. Of the 3,076 arrestees, 2,536 people were arrested for looting offenses. Of the 613 most serious cases, 344 resulted in guilty pleas (about one-half to misdemeanors), the conviction rate at trial was 7 to 1, and 107 people were sentenced to jail terms of a year or more. Of 1,742 sentences imposed by that date, 57 percent involved jail time, and 75 percent of those sentenced received an additional penalty beyond time served prior to the disposition of the case. Less than half of those sentenced on felony charges—typically burglary—received any jail time at all. A total of 988 blackout defendants were sentenced to at least some time in jail. Jail sentences, the report showed, were higher than what might ordinarily have been expected, given the charges on which the defendants were arrested.

The report also revealed "a number of differences between the results in blackout cases and those in nonblackout cases" in the Criminal Court, the lower tribunal in the court system, and additional "differences" in the Supreme Court. All persons arrested are brought to Criminal Court for the initial processing of their cases, whether they are charged with felonies or misdemeanors. Misdemeanors are handled from start to finish in Criminal Court; felony charges are tried in Supreme Court.

The "differences" were that in the Criminal Court phase of processing blackout cases, prosecutors and judges took—especially in the immediate aftermath—a tougher line than normally taken in burglary arrests, the typical charge in the blackout. But in the Supreme Court, the situation was reversed. In the Criminal Court, 50 percent of defendants convicted of blackout related offenses received jail sentences in contrast to 32 percent in a comparison group of nonblackout burglary cases. In addition, 25 percent of the cases were held for grand jury action in contrast to 6 percent in the nonblackout group.

Of jail sentences, the report stated: "The difference can be explained fully by the fact that defendants convicted of blackout related offenses served time in custody before sentencing four times more frequently than did defendants convicted of nonblackout offenses." If the trials did not ultimately produce the harsh penalties the public expected, it was because the blackout defendants had been punished before trial.

As for the high rate of cases held for the grand jury, Mr. Merola told *the New York Times,* "We were tougher on the looters, there's no question about it." The unusual toughness, however—the overall 25 percent referral rate to grand jury, compared to the more usual 6 percent rate—meant that when the blackout cases finally reached the Supreme Court, judges there were faced with cases less compelling and less convincing. "These were difficult cases," Mr. Merola added. "They were not the best type of cases from the legal point of view."[18]

THE PROLIFERATION OF POVERTY

As devastating as it was for the city, the looting at least provided a sneak preview of economic and social changes that, given the normal lag in census statistics, would not have become visible for several more years. And what the brief picture showed of the deterioration in neighborhoods and general proliferation of poverty throughout the boroughs was alarming indeed.

When darkness engulfed the city on the night of July 13, no one—not even those who claim to have predicted such an event—guessed that major destruction would have occurred in areas other than the traditionally poor neighborhoods such as Harlem, Bedford-Stuyvesant and the ever-shifting entity known as the South Bronx. And, to be sure, the settled poverty neighborhoods were hard hit. Where stores were still doing business in Mott Haven, Melrose and Morrisania—and where they were not guarded by shotgun-toting owners—they were readily looted. Third Avenue in East Harlem experienced some of the most destructive stealing in the city. And some sixteen stores were cleaned out along West 125th Street in Harlem despite, as we have noted, the fortuitous presence of a sizeable body of police.

The great surprise, however, was that just as extensive if not more thorough and destructive looting occurred in many other neighborhoods not generally associated with dense, ghetto-like poverty. As detailed in Chapter II, looting in Brooklyn occurred not only in Bedford-Stuyvesant, Browns-ville and Ocean Hill, but also extensively in Crown Heights and Bushwick, in Flatbush and East Flatbush, and in Sunset Park and Coney Island. Indeed, a Planning Department map showing the looted stores makes it seem as if fully half the borough was involved.

In the Bronx, looting went so far above what only four years before had been regarded as a major barrier to further migration of the poor—the Cross Bronx Expressway—as to envelop the Grand Concourse all the way to Fordham Road, half way up the borough.

The biggest surprise that night, though, came in Manhat-tan, where of the 348 stores looted, 155, or 44 percent, were *outside* of Harlem, East Harlem and the Lower East Side. On the West Side, from the forties to 110th Street, 87 stores were hit, more than in any other section, including East Harlem, in which only 75 were looted. Most of this looting occurred on the Upper West Side, from 59th Street to 110th Street. In this area, 61 stores were hit, which is half again as many as were struck either in Central Harlem or on the Lower East Side.

The widespread looting suggests several things, one of which is that the popular notion of the ghetto as a geograph-ically delineated area is no longer useful in marking where the poor minorities live. Using the looting to map the cutting edge of poverty migration in New York, it would seem that the poor now live pretty much throughout the Bronx, Brooklyn and Manhattan, so much so that it would be easier to say where they are *not*, rather than where they are. We have been lectured by many writers who say that the poor will always be with us. What the looting suggests is that the poor are now *neighbors* to most of us.

The looting also showed that the rate of out-migration from traditional ghetto neighborhoods has proceeded so headlong in recent years that the conventional statistical tools of analysis, such as the 1970 census, became obsolete from almost the day they were placed in use. Poverty now seems to be moving with such windlike speed that in many cases by the time a neighborhood registers a blip on the social radar, it has already deteriorated so far as to defy remediation.

In Bushwick it would have taken a sharp eye back in 1968 to have noticed the barely perceptible upcreep in fire calls for engine companies, a reliable indicator of impending social decay. But by 1972 someone should perhaps have run up a red flag when those calls hit 6,000 a year, which fire analysts see as a danger point. Nevertheless it took the devastating looting to draw people's eyes to the community. But by then, fire calls had actually begun to decline; much of what could possibly burn had already burned. The cycle running from deterioration to destruction had seen its course in six years, before anyone, except Bushwick's unfortunate residents, had noticed it.

Different neighborhoods are in different stages of change. We also recognize that generalities made about a community necessarily overlook its positive aspects and tend to err on the side of hyperbole. Nevertheless we have looked closely at a few of these transitional communities to examine how the changes have affected the quality of life there, and also to see how and in what combination the changes might have contributed to the looting during the blackout.

All the areas have exhibited most of the following characteristics:[1]

—Almost all have absorbed large numbers of minorities in the past decade. Most were overwhelmingly white in 1965 while only a few, such as Flatbush and Coney Island, remain predominantly white today.

—Several of the transitional areas were deemed too well-off to qualify for antipoverty funds when the Economic Opportunities Act was passed in 1964.

—Unlike traditional ghetto neighborhoods, where crime has in many cases dropped in recent years, almost all transitional neighborhoods have experienced sharp rises in crime since 1970.

—In all cases, either the neighborhoods had a large influx of welfare recipients, or the people already living there suffered a significant decrease in their standard of living. In either case, the neighborhoods underwent a considerable degree of economic decline.

The Upper West Side

The looting on the Upper West Side of Manhattan was perhaps the most surprising, especially to those New Yorkers who have always found—and still do find—such pleasure in the hip, earthy, intellectual and relaxed ambiance of the neighborhood. It was perhaps almost more shocking because, although the well-off professionals and professors, bureaucrats and students are surrounded by black and Hispanic poor, it never appeared that the habitués of Columbia University, Lincoln Center and the smart shops and restaurants in between had lost control of the neighborhood's style and behavior. Unlike Harlem, where whites have not moved freely since the mid-1960s, most of Broadway, Amsterdam and Columbus Avenues belong to everyone.

Nevertheless the Upper West Side has undergone many changes. In the period from 1970 to 1971, there was a significant increase in the number of cases receiving public assistance. Although in 1973 and 1974, the percentage of welfare people on the Upper West Side sharply decreased, reflecting a decline in welfare cases throughout the city, since 1974 the welfare population has steadily risen, even through 1976–1977, when the citywise welfare rolls began to decline again. Although the percentage of whites has stayed constant, between 1970 and 1974, public assistance income in the area increased by 21.4 percent, from $12,554,000 to $15,264,000, while the per capita income rose by merely 2.8 percent, from $3,236 to $3,327.

As for robbery and theft, the 24th Precinct, which serves the area from 86th Street to 110th Street, reports that crime dropped nearly 45 percent between 1971 and 1973. Since 1973, however, crime has risen almost to the point where it was in 1971.

A Brief History

What happened—and where—on the Upper West Side when the lights flickered and died on July 13 is best analyzed by first looking at developments over the last ten years. The Upper West Side refers loosely to the area from Columbus Circle to 125th Street. Its outer corridors—Riverside Drive, West End Avenue and Central Park West—maintain more or less the same middle- and upper-middle-class ambiance for most of that distance. The blocks in between, however, seem to divide themselves into five separate areas.

1) The blocks from 59th Street to 72nd Street are dominated by the cultural ambiance of Lincoln Center and the upper-middle-income apartment houses and high-priced restaurants that surround it.

2) From 72nd Street to 86th, the tone mellows slightly. Here, from the park to the river, live middle-class professionals, many of them in the renovated brownstones in the seventies and eighties between Broadway and Central Park West. They patronize the new restaurants, antique shops and boutiques which have arrived in the last three to four years.

3) From 86th Street to 96th Street, deterioration begins. For one thing, development of the urban renewal area, a ten-

block stretch between Amsterdam and Columbus, from 87th to 96th Streets, has been stymied for some ten years because power blocs in the area could not agree on what income groups would get to live in the proposed housing. The result has been severe deterioration of many buildings. When they are observed with tunnel vision, some blocks have the same bombed-out, boarded-up look of the South Bronx. Also, commercial life along Broadway begins to wither in the low nineties. Here prostitutes sell their wares, retiring into the residency hotels bordering Broadway. Smart shops and restaurants give way to the cheap stores, sidewalk merchandising, bodegas and marginal eateries that mark slum business strips.

4) From 96th Street to 110th Street is the most deteriorated section of the Upper West Side, commercially and residentially. Many stores are boarded up, unable to make a go of it with their mostly low-income customers. While Riverside Drive and West End Avenue provide some shelter for the middle class, these streets are dotted with badly run-down single-room-occupancy hotels—the "SROs." East of Broadway, stretching to Central Park, lies the thirty-block depression, both physically and socially, known locally as Manhattan Valley. The area contains about 27,000 people, most of them quite poor. A recent survey by the Manhattan Valley Development Corporation found that 30 percent of them receive some form of public assistance.[2] Recent community-board statistics claim that the rate of abandonment in Manhattan Valley is among the highest in the city, with over sixty abandoned apartment buildings listed by 1977.

About one-quarter of the residents are black, another quarter white and oriental, and one-half, Hispanic. Of the latter group, a majority are thought to be newly arrived Dominicans, a truly phantom population, many of whom are illegal aliens not attached to any permanent institutions and by all accounts desperately poor. Diane Morales, president of School Board No. 3, says that more than half the students in P.S. 165 on 109th Street are now Dominican, as are a majority of mothers using the prenatal care clinic at the Neighborhood Health Services Program, 106 W. 100th St., where Ms. Morales is the council coordinator. They use the clinic, she said, because it asks no questions and considers a mother's need as the only qualification for receiving service.

5) From 110th Street, prosperity returns abruptly, as Columbia and other institutions on Morningside Heights and Riverside Drive invigorate both commercial and residential life of the neighborhood almost all the way to 125th Street.

* * *

How much housing should be built for the poor or the non-poor provides most of the controversy for political battles on the Upper West Side. In the past ten years, this area has experienced a middle-class resurgence that is rare in New York City. Beginning with the construction of Lincoln Center and its attendant high-rise housing on West End Avenue during the 1960s, and carried northward by shop owners, brownstone owners, and powerful real estate interests, the process of gentrification seems to have gone well beyond the stages of a fadish trend, into an established fact. Near Sherman Square at 72nd street, which a 1965 *Life* Magazine article referred to as "Needle Park,"[3] and along 85th Street between West End and Riverside, which during the Lindsay years won a media reputation as the "worst block in Manhattan," renovated brownstones now go for $250,000, rents for two bedroom apartments begin at about $500, and the middle, and upper-middle classes seem to have set their feet to stay.

For the poor, however, the concomitant of the upgrading in the sixties, seventies and eighties has been a general uprooting and compaction into the nineties and hundreds to the north.

Both Lincoln Center and the West Side Urban Renewal Area (WSURA) resulted in the dislocation of thousands of poor and working-class families. Estimates of the number disrupted by WSURA run as high as 12,000 families. There were almost 6,000 relocatees identified by the city at the time it acquired buildings in the area, but this did not include hundreds living in SROs on the site, and many more dispersed prior to acquisition by the familiar process of deterioration that accompanies designation of an area as a renewal site. Almost 2,000 of these relocatees were eventually placed in new or rehabilitated housing on WSURA, a percentage that is significantly higher than other renewal areas in New York.

WSURA, the largest renewal project in the country when designated in 1962, has transformed the central part of the West Side. By the night of the blackout, 11,348 units of housing had been built, rehabilitated or renovated in the renewal area. By all estimates, no more than 23 percent of these units are occupied by low-income residents. Thousands of other poor people were dispersed throughout the West Side and the city, their housing taken over by a mixture that strongly emphasized moderate- and middle-income development as well as rehabilitated, upper-middle-income brownstones.

The center axis from Broadway to Amsterdam to Columbus Avenues has steadily absorbed more of the poor, the unemployed and welfare populations which have become isolated from the affluence along the exterior lanes of Riverside Drive, West End Avenue and Central Park West.

"What we've done," says Ira Kornbluh, a political leader in the area and a chairman of Planning Board #7, "is to solve the problems of the lower part of the district at the expense of the upper."

The process of gentrification, however, has not proceeded unopposed, as any witness to the raucous planning board meetings can testify. Housing and social action groups, such as the Stryckers Bay Neighborhood Association, Goddard Riverside Community Center and the Manhattan Valley Development Corporation, have helped the poor resist their evacuation from the area and have tried to capture a large portion of the new housing that will be built on urban renewal sites.

The Manhattan Valley Development Corporation is convinced that the market for middle-class housing is so strong, in fact, that even its own thoroughly run-down bailiwick would fall to real estate developers if it eased its vigilance. "If we hadn't been here, the poor would have been pushed out long ago,'' says Leigh Schneider, a director of the group which operates a number of sweat-equity rehabilitation projects in the district.

"From many viewpoints Manhattan Valley is the last 'plum' to be picked by the real estate operators who are increasingly dominating the economics of the housing market on the Upper West Side,'' reads the group's pamphlet. "Several buildings in Manhattan Valley have already been converted by private landlords into comparatively high-rent housing and several others would have been, had it not been for the vigilance of the MVDC along with other neighborhood groups insisting that private rehabilitation efforts provide apartments for low-income families.''

On the opposite side, along with real-estate interests and the general business community are block groups such as the United Federation of West Side Block Associations and an aggressive organization called CONTINUE, which says it represents 3,000 brownstone owners. "Everything can't be for low-income groups in this city,'' says Ira Haldenstein, the preeminent brownstone realtor and booster in the area. "The middle class has to have somewhere to go.'' He sees the brownstoners as a stabilizing force—indeed, as the true saviors of the Upper West Side for the middle class. "They earn about $80,000, $90,000 a year—that's both husband and wife working. They spend a lot of money. They send their children to private school. They eat out in restaurants. They're a tremendous boon to any area.'' While brownstone bargains in the sixties, seventies and eighties are all but gone, the demand is pushing up into the nineties. His only problem, he says, is a shortage of brownstone houses. "Anything I can get my hands on I can sell,'' he said.

Needless to say, there is hardly any issue on which groups like Stryckers Bay and CONTINUE can agree. They not only don't agree on how many new low-income units should be built in WSURA, but they are also far apart on the number already built. CONTINUE contends that WSURA already contains more than the 2,500 units guaranteed under the renewal plan, while Strycker's claims WSURA is hundreds of units short of the goal for low-income units.

The conflict over what to do with the 9 remaining urban renewal parcels has split the Community Planning Board down the middle. Each major issue has been decided by a single vote by committees with up to 17 members. CONTINUE has pulled along with it other, more moderate, community leaders, and has gotten much of what it wanted in the final Board plan. Strycker's and the United Tenant Association, a newly formed organization which claims to represent the 200 on-site tenant families, forced some concessions—including a Board resolution guaranteeing that all of the federally subsidized apartments on the new sites will be given to tenants in the lower range of the federal income limits, which is approximately $8,000 a year.

As the debate continues, it adds an ironic note if we look at the issues in light of the original phrasing of the 1958 City Planning Commission report which laid the groundwork for the designation of WSURA:

This is not only a plan to provide housing and reverse the trend of neighborhood deterioration, but to establish a new kind of urban environment in a strategic and congested section of the city offering pleasant and varied living conditions for a broad cross section of the population. Its vision is of an entire neighborhood truly integrated (economically, culturally, and ethnically) on a stable basis, not simply caught at the point where there is apparent integration while one group is moving in and another out.[4]

The SROs

The poor of Manhattan Valley and those of the central axis of Columbus and Amsterdam Avenues consist largely of families with children. An entirely different kind of poor has concentrated itself in the Single Room Occupancy hotels and rooming houses off Broadway in the nineties and hundreds. The 65 or 70 SRO hotels on the West Side were created from apartment houses in the Depression years and until the late fifties provided "respectable" housing for single, mostly older whites. They contain anywhere from 50 to 450 rooms which rent for between $100 and $150 a month, depending usually on whether there is a private bath. Shared kitchen arrangements are also common.

SRO occupants consist of several different populations. Some are the elderly, mostly white, who can only afford single rooms on their limited pension or social security checks. Some are men and women with problems, such as alcoholism, who live on public assistance. Another group, a considerable one, are deinstitutionalized mental patients who have been discharged from city and state hospitals after being diagnosed as harmless to themselves and others. The latter population, although not a serious crime threat, has been particularly disconcerting to West Siders who see their presence on Broadway as contributing to the general seediness of the area. Indeed, a person returning to the Upper West Side after an absence of five years might well perceive a slight increase in the traditional complement of paper-bag ladies, lurching tramps and strollers engaged in angry self-dialogue.

Another SRO contingent presents a substantially larger problem when it comes to the crime rate. This includes releasees, largely black, from prisons on Riker's Island. They are steered by counselors to SRO hotels both in the Times Square area and the Upper West Side to begin life anew. It also includes an assortment of drug addicts, ex-addicts on methadone, pimps, prostitutes and other small-time criminals.

Precisely what representation each group has in the whole SRO population is impossible to pinpoint. Neither is it possible to say definitely what effect the criminally-oriented group has on burglaries and muggings on the Upper West Side. Suffice it to say that the police visit the SROs far more often than the representation of their occupants in the general population would warrant.

At night some of the SROs send vibrations out into the

general community that are impossible to ignore. Patricia
Koce, for instance, president of the West 94th Street Block
Association, lives in back of the Vancouver, located on a West-
side block between Riverside Drive and West End Avenue. The block is particularly notorious because besides the
Vancouver, it contains five other SROs. One of the few legitimate apartment buildings, number 305, is now empty, gutted
by a fire two years ago that resulted in thirteen deaths.

"You wouldn't believe it," said Ms. Koce about what
goes on at the Vancouver.

Screaming at night, like people getting killed. 'Help! Help! Help!'
We call the precinct all the time, but we don't know which room it's
from. Stuff flying out of the windows, whole pieces of furniture. I
mean dressers and drawers, everything. I've seen cats thrown out.
And burglars. We watch burglars climbing through the fire escapes,
and we call the police, but I don't know if they ever get caught. People masturbating—standing in the windows, on the fire escape, on
the roof, day or night, it doesn't matter to them.

If SROs are an unwelcome presence in the neighborhood
around them, inside the hotels house a nether world that com-
bines something from Saroyan, Dante and Hieronymus
Bosch. One of the better ones in the 90s is owned by a tough,
bull-necked Rumanian named Otto Schwartz, aged 70, who
said he spent three and a half years in Auschwitz before es-
caping while being transported to another camp in 1945. When
he tries to write, his right hand twitches nearly uncontrolla-
bly—the heritage, he said, of a severe clubbing in the camp.

While many SROs are run by leasees who pay upwards of
$150,000 a year to the owner for twenty to thirty-year leases,
Schwartz has owned the hotel since the early 1950s and acts
as his own concierge. One-third of his roomers are elderly, he
guesses. "The rest are small-time criminals and petty
thieves." His relationship to them seems more like a jailer
than a landlord. "Here we keep it pretty tight," he says in a
heavy European accent. No visitors are allowed after 11 P.M.
Even swearing is forbidden. "You cannot allow them the feeling that you are scared of them," says Schwartz, who stated

that he has had to kick some of his tenants to enforce deco-
rum. "You cannot allow them to use foul language or to yell
and carry on in front of the other tenants. The others will not
respect you if you let them get away with it." A Doberman
Pinscher dog named Buck does back-up duty behind a glass
door in the lobby in the event that Schwartz meets more than
his match.

He conducts business from behind a counter in a dimly lit,
garishly painted lobby. While he talks, a constant stream of
people from the SRO world moves through the small foyer to
and from the elevator, stopping to pay bills or simply to stand
awhile and then move off. Among them are brightly daubed
transvestites, prostitutes, pimps and others whose lives are
hard and filled with confusion and defeat. An old alcoholic
makes his way past the desk, his eyes watery and dazed, his
mouth open in a sort of permanent expression of bewilder-
ment. A woman approaching the desk is so full of depressant
she cannot open her eyes; words barely escape from her
mouth. "You should see her when she's off the stuff," says
Schwartz. "She's so wild you can't hold her down."

About three-quarters of the traffic is black, the rest Hispanic and white. Now and then an elderly person gingerly
threads his or her way through the throng. A more or less permanent fixture in the lobby is an old black man called
"Professor," who brandishes a red and white blind-man's
cane, yet whose eyes have the disconcerting habit of following everyone's movements. "Don't let him fool you,"
Schwartz says when Professor is out of hearing. "He can pick
pennies off the floor in the dark.

Nearly everyone in the hotel subsists on some form of
government check—aid to the disabled for methadone addicts
and released mental patients, social security for the old. The
postman brings the checks on the first and the fifteenth of every month to Schwartz, who acts as paymaster and makes
tenants settle up for the rent before he hands over the checks.
"You give them the check, only you give it to them like this,"
he says, clamping a large thumb down on one corner of the
envelope. On the day we talked to him, Schwartz had to send

an assistant to Riker's Island with some of the checks in order to get rent from tenants temporarily housed by the Department of Corrections.

While he puts up a tough exterior, he has also given some favored tenants, such as the Professor, free room when they had no money, then refused to accept any payment when they got their checks. For some, he has also posted bail. His largesse, of course, helps to maintain his control. He explained that with new tenants he frequently offers to lend them money should they run out before check day. On the first of the month they must pay him back, which then makes them short again before the 15th, and they have to keep borrowing. "I try always to have my clientele think they need me, not that I need them," he said. "You have to have some kind of leverage on them always. There's not one of them who doesn't owe me a favor. The place is possible to run only as long as you keep tight control of it."

To do this, Schwartz found he had to live on the premises himself, along with his wife and, until she married recently, his daughter. Even his short absence away from the hotel can unleash problems. "Once," he said, "I snuck away for a weekend, and when I came back they were jumping all over the place. It took me two days to calm them down."

With it all, the SRO has made Schwartz a more than comfortable living. His gross income is about $250,000, he said. His staff of nine consists mostly of tenants who are not paid high wages. After paying for heat, light and taxes, the balance is his. When he began in the business, he said, the SROs were run "99 percent" by Jews who came from Europe because of the war. Now the ownership is changing. "The old people are getting fat. They're getting out. They don't want to stay around and deal with the bums you have to deal with here." The new owners tend to be Koreans, Indians, Chinese from Hong Kong, and Hispanics. Shortly, he plans to sell out himself and move to a house he owns in the Catskills.

"I'm really a great admirer of peace and quiet," he said. "For me the turbulence is over. I've been running since 1939, and soon it's time to stop."

* * *

While most people agree that SROs are a problem, no one has yet come up with a workable solution. The city's Office of SRO Housing is a self-admitted "finger in the dike operation." What's more, it sees its job as that of advocate for SRO tenants, rather than for the community—a dedication which earns little admiration from middle-class West Siders.

Some private groups have organized special residences for the elderly to get them away from predatory tenants of SROs. Others have tried to install social services in SROs to help tenants cope with life successfully. Both efforts are expensive and hence limited. "Frankly," said Murray Siegel, president of the West Side Chamber of Commerce, in a fairly representative opinion, "I'm not interested in giving 'services' to them. I'm interested only in getting them the hell out of here."

There are signs that Siegel may be slowly getting his wish, at least in the renovated blocks of the seventies and eighties. Here the bull market for middle- and upper-middle-income housing has influenced owners of several SROs to clear out their low-income tenantry and renovate the buildings into classier apartment houses. Encouraging this trend is the city's J51 tax law, which gives a 90 percent tax abatement for ten years on the cost of the renovation. Through this approach some of the most notorious SROs, such as the West Towers on 76th Street and the Endicott Hotel on Columbus Avenues opposite the American Museum of Natural History, have become or are becoming middle-income or luxury housing. A budding business has been developed for "evacuators," or eviction lawyers who specialize in clearing tenants out of the path of renovation.

Just when—or indeed, whether—this trend will reach into the blocks along Broadway in the nineties and hundreds, only time will tell. Some people think it is only a matter of three to five years before the rental market becomes strong enough so that J51 renovations become economically feasible there. Others, such as Siegel of the Chamber of Commerce, think something must first happen to the great vacant lot at 96th Street and Broadway in order to bring the area's commerce back to life. The lot was to have been the site of a new Alexander's store which, in a now generally lamented decision, was voted down by the Planning Board in 1969. After that, the lot was taken over by one developer who failed to come up with a workable plan. Now another one, Starrett City, has charge, but so far no plan has come forth. One thing the planning board has refused to allow on the site, is low-income housing.

The Looting

To people who watched it, the looting on the Upper West Side seemed to have little of the carnival glee associated with other areas. Various people we interviewed said it contained elements of mass hysteria tinged with a slightly threatening air. Diane Morales, chairman of Community School Board No. 3, was at a board meeting when the lights went out. She had to walk across 96th Street from West End to Columbus as people swarmed into the streets. "In the last blackout," she said,

I walked from CCNY down to here and I felt nothing that was threatening. But this time there was a bad feeling in the air. I can't describe it, quite. This time I felt it was not healthy to be out. Kids with mopeds were racing around crazily, going right up on the sidewalk. There was a lot of harrassing of people who were walking. Last time there were people directing traffic, trying to help each other. This time it was everyone out for themselves.

As we will detail below, the looting on the Upper West Side, similar to the pattern in other neighborhoods, tended to be initiated by criminally oriented street people, who were then joined by thousands of normally law-abiding poor people whose moral constraints were temporarily removed by the mood of the street and the seductive opportunities that suddenly came their way.

Of the 61 stores looted on the Upper West Side between 63rd and 110th Streets, 39 were on Broadway, 16 on Amsterdam and 6 on Columbus. Of the Broadway stores, all but 9 were located in the 20-block stretch between 90th and 110th Streets. On Amsterdam, all those hit were located in the same stretch. Manhattan Valley experienced very little looting because most of its commercial establishments are bars, second-hand stores, bodegas and laundromats, which were generally not touched that night.[5]

The looting on Amsterdam and Columbus Avenues differed from that on Broadway in that from all accounts it was much more like a family project, rather than one that drew groups of unattached males.

Joe and Susan Feldstein—he is a thirty-seven-year-old advertising executive and she is a thirty-one-year-old television producer—were having a dinner party that night in their apartment overlooking Amsterdam Avenue at 93rd Street. They watched, horrified, from the first smashed window until 3:30 A.M., when they finally went to bed.

"When the lights went out, there was a roar in the street, like it was a stadium," says Feldstein. There were yells, whistles, and screaming, but nothing more, for what he guesses was about fifteen minutes. Then he heard the first glass breaking. "I ran to the window and there were these four guys, Spanish guys, with golf clubs. They were coming up the sidewalk from farther downtown tapping store windows out as they went. Just 'tap' and 'crash,' the windows broke, one after another." The four men did not take anything, Feldstein said, but their window breaking seemed to create excitement among people watching. Suddenly, he said, floods of people were running out of the public housing project on Amsterdam at 93rd Street. "They poured out of the building in hordes," he said. "Mothers, fathers, children, everyone." More yelling in the street, then a cheer, and he heard the sound of metal being ripped away from a building. He saw a large American-made car pulling off the gates of the Capri Furniture store at

92nd Street. The gate came off as easily as wrapping from a cigarette package. Quickly the crowd smashed the plate-glass windows across the front of the store and flooded inside.

At that, Feldstein called 911 to get the police. The number was busy. He tried to call the 24th Precinct. Also busy. He called the 19th Precinct on the East Side to have them alert the 24th, but a policeman there said nothing could be done.

It was then, he said, that he and his wife began to feel thoroughly scared.

The thing that really upset me was here I was calling to report looting and rioting, and I could not get through. What if I was in the middle of the looting and rioting myself? They could have burned our building down, they could have stormed the building, killed people, and I had no way of getting the police. That's what was really scary—the total absence of law and order or anything. We felt isolated, cut off.

By now, he said, it was about 10:30 and the looting was general, not only in the Capri store but at a shoe store across the way. Whole families were carrying stolen furniture into the housing project and down side streets. What the owner later said would have taken him two trucks and a whole week to deliver was carried off in two or three hours. Women had pairs of matched lamps. Men carried sofas; children would help with the pillows and small end tables. One woman, a large black lady with knee-high white jeans whom the Feldsteins recognized as living in the project, was jumping up and down like a cheerleader, urging the people into the store, shouting hurrahs when they came out with some goods. "Go get it, yeh, yeh!" she shouted.

Feldstein and his wife watched until 3:30 A.M., mainly because they were afraid of fire. Many people had candles; some had handmade torches and kerosene lanterns.

"And all that time we watched, we never saw one person get arrested," he said. "Police cars would come by every fifteen or twenty minutes and the looters would just run out of the store to the corner and wait until the police left. Then they'd go back into the store for more."

Watching the looting deeply changed the Feldsteins' perception about their neighborhood. "I've lived here for seven years, and we've always known it's not a safe area," he said. "We've had robberies, a murder on the block—all that. But we never really felt threatened before. It was the first time we've seen such mob violence. . . ."

Up at the 24th Precinct, the police were having their own troubles, with only eight squad cars plus a few unmarked detective cars to patrol an area of 125 square blocks. In addition, the precinct's emergency generator had broken down two weeks before and had never been fixed. This meant that not only was walkie-talkie communication dead between the men on the street and the precinct, but the station house had to operate with flashlights and candles like everyone else. While stalled elevators were not much of a problem on the West Side, one sergeant was stuck in the precinct house elevator for two hours before he was freed.

When the lights went out, Sgt. Freud, supervisor of patrol, put his available cars on the main commercial strips. He and his driver started down Broadway. At 9:45 he encountered the first looting, at 98th Street, where some sixty to seventy men were pulling down the gates of the Radio Clinic "with their bare hands." Sgt. Freud addressed the crowd over his loudspeaker atop the cruiser. "I told them, 'I'm asking you to disperse, go to your homes, this is your community' and things like that, trying to solicit their cooperation."

Their cooperation was not forthcoming. The sergeant's message was greeted with a hail of bottles; one man picked up a trash basket and threw it at the police car. At this, Sgt. Freud decided discretion was the better part of valor. "I advised my chauffeur," he said, "to proceed down to 96th Street, as to stay around would have been foolhardy." He radioed to central headquarters for backup units but failed to get through. It was then that the sergeant, like the advertising man, realized how much he was alone that night.

As it turned out, the police of the 24th Precinct made more than the average number of arrests. Not only did its men pick up a total of 140 looting suspects, more than most precincts, but they arrested more people earlier than anyone else. By 12:30 that night, the 24th had pulled in 25 percent of its arrestees, while, as noted in Chapter V, the police average for the city by this time was only 7 percent. This still meant that the large-scale looters stood the best chance of getting away. From accounts by policemen themselves, it would appear that most break-ins on the Upper West Side were made by 11:00 P.M. Anyone still out after midnight was, in the word of one patrolman, a "scavenger," and not a prime beneficiary of the night's work.

Of the 140 arrestees, 78 were black, 60 were Hispanic and 2, quite probably, were white. Of the blacks, 30 came from blocks in the nineties and hundreds west of Broadway, 27 came from east of Broadway (of these, 12 gave addresses in Manhattan Valley, above 100th Street), 8 were from the eighties and nineties, and 7 lived in public housing on Amsterdam and Columbus Avenues. The rest, 21, gave addresses in other parts of the city.[6]

The Hispanic arrestees were more generally distributed. Eighteen came from Amsterdam and Columbus Avenues; 14, from blocks in the nineties east of Broadway; 11, from Manhattan Valley; and 6, from other parts of the city.

While we recognize the problems inherent in making generalizations about the looters from the arrest statistics, it is still possible to come to several tentative conclusions about who did what on the Upper West Side. First, it seems pretty clear that, generally, blacks hit Broadway, and Hispanics, Amsterdam and Columbus Avenues. Of the 68 arrests on Broadway, 50 were blacks; only 18 were Hispanic. Conversely, of the arrests everywhere else, mostly on Amsterdam and Columbus, 33 were Hispanic and 18 were black.[7]

Second, while it is impossible to prove it beyond a doubt, strong evidence exists that many of the stores on Broadway were initially opened by the rootless, criminally-prone male population that lives in the SRO hotels near Broadway in the nineties and hundreds. We came to this conclusion, not by giving credence to the conjecture of store owners—although there was plenty of that—but by analyzing the times when certain arrests were made on Broadway.

Overall only 22 of the 140 arrestees gave their addresses as an SRO hotel. Yet while 25 percent of the overall 140 figure were arrested before 12:30 A.M., fully 73 percent of the SRO arrestees, or nearly three times as many, were picked up before 12:30 A.M. What's more, in the first hour, 33 percent of the SRO arrestee population was picked up, as opposed to only 8.5 percent of the general arrestees. This would tally with the theory that on a hot night in July, the SRO population of petty criminals would be out on the street corner, ready and more willing than most people to take immediate advantage of the blackout—and, consequently, to run a greater chance of getting picked up by the 24th Precinct where the police made more than three times the average number of early arrests.

Further examination of the arrest statistics yields more evidence. While the 22 SRO arrestees added to only 15 percent of the total picked up that night, they accounted for *42 percent* of all those arrested on Broadway during the first three hours of the looting. Put another way, during the time that the greatest amount of looting was going on, and on the street that was the most heavily looted, almost half of those arrested turned out to be SRO occupants. All the rest of the night and into the next day, when 75 percent of the total arrests were made of "scavengers," as the police called them, the SRO arrestees accounted for only 8 percent of the total.

Evidence pointing to the involvement of another population group that night is not as conclusive as it is merely interesting. Looking at the 61 arrestees with Hispanic surnames, we suspect that a significant minority may well be Dominican. We gave the arrest list independently to two Dominican activists, the Reverend Ricardo Potter, a staff associate at the National Council of Churches, and Cotubanama Dipp, who heads the Dominican Manpower Project on 90th Street and Broadway, the only Dominican antipoverty organization in the city. Mr. Potter chose 10 names as "probably" Dominican; Dipp chose 20. This is hardly decisive evidence that between 17 percent and 30 percent of the Hispanic looters came from among the rootless Dominican population. It merely provides a suspicion that deserves further investigation.

Another interesting footnote: the only large supermarket to be heavily looted on the Upper West Side was the Foodo-rama on Broadway at 104th Street. The store is opposite the Regent Hotel at 104th Street, which is a large, temporary residence for "burn-outs": welfare families, mostly women and children, who have been burned out of their apartments elsewhere in the city and are waiting to find other places to live.

Bushwick

Bushwick illuminates most clearly our view that what occurred during the blackout was foreshadowed by the character of the community and patterns of behavior that prevailed before the lights went out. Bushwick is significant also in that it illustrates the complete cycle, from delapidation to decay to destruction by fire, that had occurred previously in areas of the South Bronx. Not all of the changing neighborhoods we have discussed are clearly headed for the fate of Bushwick. But some, particularly in the west Bronx, may very well be.

In 1964, when federal legislation was passed establishing the Anti-Poverty Programs in large cities, Bushwick in Brooklyn was not considered eligible, although some deterioration had already begun to set in. The changes, however, were inchoate and not yet visible to the bureaucrats who considered it then a fairly stable, working-class community. Few, if any, could predict that in 1977 it would become, as Paul Delaney of *The New York Times* called it, "a gauge of the typical slum of the seventies."[8] Changes in Bushwick were sweeping even in the sixties, when the area lost one-third of its population and the black and Hispanic population increased from 24,703 to 80,569, a change of 232 percent. Now 50 percent of the area's approximately 100,000 residents are Hispanic and 40 percent black, with the remaining 10 percent comprising a small, working-class Italian enclave in the north, on the Queens border.

In 1970 Bushwick was not as severely depressed as some of the other neighborhoods in central Brooklyn, such as Ocean Hill-Brownsville and East New York. But in the 1970s the pace of decay and deterioration accelerated tremendously. A warning should have been sounded two years later, in 1972, when fire engine companies began exceeding the magic number of 6,000 runs a year, a volume regarded as signifying severe social problems. In 1977, Ladder Companies 124 and 112, which sit side by side on Hemrod Street in Bushwick, were number *one* and *two* in the city, although fires in the district are now beginning to trail off.

The increase in crime in the area since 1971 is astonishing: between 1971 and 1975, robberies more than doubled, burglaries increased by 40 percent and grand larceny rose by more than 100 percent.[9] In 1976 the 83rd Precinct in Bushwick handled more crime than any other command in central Brooklyn. While city officials have pressed the federal government to declare the city a disaster area because of the blackout looting, Bushwick had clearly achieved disaster status by the night before the blackout.

Much has been written about fear of crime among ghetto residents, but in Bushwick it is shared equally by the businessmen, who are especially hard hit. Truck drivers making deliveries to stores routinely head first for the 83rd Precinct to get a police escort. The police reported that some department stores, such as Sears, have simply stopped delivering merchandise in the area, and require customers to pick it up at the store.

Every store owner along Broadway has his long tale of woe. In fact the tenacity with which they stay in business, despite the plethora of hold-ups and burglaries, seems evidence itself that at least some profit is being derived. Liquor stores find they have to become especially well-fortified to survive. At one Broadway establishment, a customer must walk down

(% change)

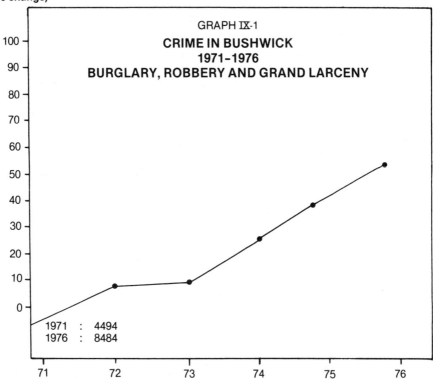

GRAPH IX-1
CRIME IN BUSHWICK
1971–1976
BURGLARY, ROBBERY AND GRAND LARCENY

1971 : 4494
1976 : 8484

Source: New York City Police Department, *Statistical Report:*
Complaint and Arrests, 1971–1976.

an alleyway lined by ten feet of bullet-proof glass. To give his order, he has to bend down and speak to the proprietor through the money slot. Instead of keeping a gun hidden under the counter as most liquor dealers do, the owner, who has had the store for thirty years, wears it conspicuously on his hip. This display of arms, however, was not sufficient to deter two men who walked up to him on the street as he was going to the bank with the day's receipts a year or two ago, poked a gun in his face, and held him up. "I had a bad pattern then of always going to the bank at the same time," the man said. "But now I've changed that." When taking money to the bank he draws his gun and carries it in his hand like a Brinks guard. The night of the looting, the owner was in his store, looking out at the street from a peephole in his metal sheathing, armed with his revolver, a shotgun and a large vicious dog. He was not touched.

Arson

Of all the looted areas, Bushwick burned the brightest that night. At one point, said Chief Schochet of the 37th Battalion, Broadway was involved in "mass conflagration." Two solid blocks were going up in flames from fires in two four-story buildings and a large five-and-ten which burned to the ground. Early in the evening, Chief Schochet called WINS to counter reports over the radio station that people were reacting to the blackout with the same calm they had in 1965. When he told a reporter of the looting and burning in Bushwick, the reporter asked him, "Where's that?"

The next day it was even worse, he said, with numerous multiple alarms, including one in a seven-story knitting mill and in several other factories, one of which arsonists finally succeeded in destroying after firemen tried repeatedly to save it. At one point the elevated subway line on Broadway had to be shut down for fear that the charred buildings lining the tracks would collapse on the trains.

But while Bushwick shocked people with its high incidence of arson during the blackout, the community seemed only to be doing what it normally does, only much more of it.

Burning down buildings, as Frank Puig, chairman of Community Board No. 4, said about the South Bronx, has become "part of the culture." While nationally the arson rate fluctuates between 15 and 20 percent of structural fires, in Bushwick last year the best estimates by local fire officials put it at a little over 75 percent. Of the 1,730 fires, 1,315 were ruled "suspicious." Of these, 1,038 were in abandoned buildings; 277 were in occupied structures.[10] With a total of 6,472 fire runs a year, Ladder 124 in Bushwick dealt with more calls than the fire department of the city of Vienna. This is according to Paul DeCicco, director of the Environmental Urban Studies at the Polytechnic Institute of New York in Brooklyn.

Mr. DeCicco began studying Bushwick fires back in 1972, the point at which the community virtually started burning down. Of the 12,000 structures in Bushwick, between 1,500 and 1,700 suffer fire damage each year, and more often than not the buildings never recover. Down Central Avenue, which courses through all the community's twenty-four blocks, no side street exists that does not house at least one burned structure. Driving around with Battalion Chief Edward Borst, we realized that it was possible to see the course of burning and even to predict which buildings will go next.

Ten months before the blackout, Harmon Street, between Wilson and Central Avenues, had only two or three burned buildings on it. By the summer of 1977 it was two-thirds burned and abandoned. Greene Street, also between Central and Wilson Avenues, was even more burned down, with only three buildings occupied out of thirty. A commercial strip on Wilson Avenue between Grove and Linden Streets had eight stores and thirty-two apartments occupied in 1976. A year later it was completely deserted.

The way it generally happens, said Chief Borst, as we

looked at a block-long row of burned-out buildings on Madison Street between Central and Wilson Avenues, is as follows:

In the winter of 1976 a fire started in the end building on Madison Street and burned it down completely, also slightly damaging one apartment in the second building. The family in that apartment moved and left it vacant. Shortly thereafter a fire started in the abandoned apartment, burned the second building down completely, and caused damage in a third. People in the third then moved out, and so on. When an abandoned building is set afire, the Fire Department goes less than all out to extinguish it—largely so as not to endanger its men. "Basically," says Chief Borst, "we treat it like a garbage fire and try not to let it spread."

Part of the reason for the fire rate in Bushwick is structural. According to Mr. DeCicco, half of the 12,000 buildings are made of wood, and many of these are covered in asphalt siding, which burns fast and gives off a lot of heat. Most of the housing stock consists of "old law" structures with air shafts over the toilets and the stairwells; these shafts act as efficient chimneys for fires started below. Because of their design, the buildings burn virtually like furnaces. In addition, few of them have fire-retardant walls between the air space, or "cockloft," which is between the roof and the top floor ceiling, and the roof itself. Thus a fire in one building can easily move laterally into another. "That's why when one goes here, they all go," DeCicco said.

Once a fire is started it is hard to stop, largely because the Fire Department cannot possibly get there in time. In a series of recent fire tests, DeCicco used the fire-starting materials available to any vandal; he succeeded quickly in completely enveloping in flames the whole side and back wall of a house. In only two minutes the flames had reached 1,500 degrees, or not far below the heat of a blast furnace. When he lit a gasoline fire in a front hall—a common way of committing arson—the whole stairway was "involved" within seconds. Yet it takes the average fire company three minutes to reach a fire and put itself into operation, he said.

In his study of Bushwick fires, DeCicco also lists six "social causes" of the fire rate:

1) Unemployment.
2) Lack of recreation facilities for young people.
3) Unfavorable demographics: Bushwick has a plethora of old and young people, and a dearth of middle-age working couples to add stability to the area.
4) The synergistic effect of high rates of smoking and alcoholism.
5) Lack of prompt sanitation service, which leaves rubbish piled near buildings. It functions as ready tinder.
6) Ethnic characteristics: "There is no doubt," said DeCicco (speaking, he emphasized, as an Italian), "that Latin blood is more volatile and revenge modes more pronounced. It's impossible to measure this factor, but all I know is, Norwegians don't do this sort of thing."

Arson is also committed for money, of course, both in apartment-house fires and in businesses, but how much, is difficult to measure. In addition it has been suggested by several people we've talked to that the extra benefits provided by the city's Welfare Department for burned-out families (these benefits include money for some types of furniture, a security deposit for a new apartment, and a finder's fee), encourage many people to burn themselves out. While undoubtedly several such cases exist, we feel it is one of those legends that gets repeated and repeated in the ghetto until it assumes proportions far removed from reality.

A final note: At one point during his fire experiments in Bushwick, Mr. DeCicco, a fortyish, professorial-looking gentleman, was fumbling with matches and a pile of paper and wood scraps, trying to get a fire started along the wall of one abandoned building. Moved by such a spectacle of ineptitude, a local resident who had been watching the scene ambled over and said: "Here, man, let me show you how to do that."

The Bronx

Our view that the patterns of change occurring prior to the blackout provided a bellwether for what happened when the lights went out is just as clear in the Bronx as on the Upper West Side or in Bushwick. Here the evidence of poor people migrating from the southern borough to the west and the north is dramatic. In Hunts Point, Mott Haven and areas a little to the north, where three or four years ago a visitor was struck by the horrendous poverty, the impression now is of a ghost city. Along 140th and 141st Streets, burned-out and empty buildings look out on empty vacant lots. The children who once played there seem to be all gone. Along Intervale Avenue in the Seabury section, all the stores are closed; on block after block there is nothing to buy but beer and soda. Unkempt, wild dogs can be seen running in packs of three or four through the deserted streets. In the old Bathgate section, the city has spent several million dollars to refurbish playgrounds in Crotona Park, but the adjacent buildings are mostly sealed-up and abandoned; few children exist to use the wealth of swings and slides.

Hunts Point's population decreased from 107,040 in 1970 to about 69,000 today, and Mott Haven has lost half its 1960 population of 126,000, with many of those who made the exodus, crowding into neighborhoods to the north and the west. These areas in turn have also lost people since 1970, as the whites and middle-class have escaped the onrushing black and Hispanic poor. Morris Heights picked up in population by 4.5 percent from 44,000 in 1970 to 46,000, but also showed a decline in taxable income of 8 percent from $88 million to $81 million. In addition it showed an increase of 138 percent for persons on welfare between 1970 and 1976 from 7,304 to 17,430. In the Mount Hope neighborhood the population increased by 3.9 percent, from 43,000 to 44,750, in the five years from 1970 to 1975; again, however, the number of persons receiving public assistance soared by 191.1 percent from 4,600 to 13,400. In the same period, Highbridge, a neighborhood just below the Cross Bronx Expressway in the West Bronx, lost about 4 percent of its 41,590 residents, while taxable income there dropped 11 percent from $76 to $68 million. Highbridge's welfare population jumped 78 percent from 8,350 to 14,872 between 1970 and 1976.

These shifts in the poor population from the South to the Central Bronx are most obvious in the changes in crime rates for the area from 1971 to 1976, compared to the west and more central area of the borough. As Graph IX-2 illustrates, when the poor migrated from areas of the South Bronx to Highbridge, Morris Heights and East Tremont, crime moved with them. While crime in Hunts Point decreased by better than 50 percent from 1971 to 1976, crime in Highbridge shot up by 30 percent. In fact, with crime declining, people moving out and buildings ending up gutted and demolished, the 41st Precinct in Hunts Point has changed its name from "Fort Apache" to "Little House on the Prairie." The new "Fort Apache" is now the 44th Precinct in Highbridge.

Frank Puig, chairman of Planning Board No. 4, forecasts a steady and rapid rate of decline in the central and northern Bronx. "The fires are already beginning," he said. "This area will look like Mott Haven and Hunts Point."

It is difficult to pinpoint exactly when the poor began crossing the old barrier of the Cross Bronx Expressway on their northward trek. Most observers, including Puig and Ed Korn of the Bronx Jewish Community Council, say it began between 1970 and 1972. But once the boundary was traversed, deterioration moved with jet-age speed. Today the poor dominate neighborhoods on both sides of the Grand Concourse— Morris Heights and University Heights on the west, Tremont and East Tremont on the east—all the way up to Fordham Road.

Deterioration in the area was significantly affected by two important developments. One was the sale of the New York University campus in University Heights to the City University system; the other was the construction of Co-op City in the northeastern corner of the borough. The sale of NYU weak-

(% change)

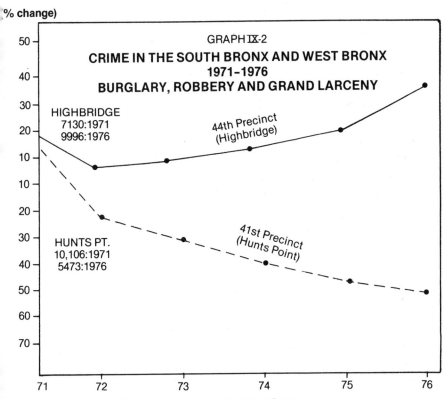

GRAPH IX-2

CRIME IN THE SOUTH BRONX AND WEST BRONX
1971–1976
BURGLARY, ROBBERY AND GRAND LARCENY

HIGHBRIDGE
7130:1971
9996:1976

44th Precinct
(Highbridge)

HUNTS PT.
10,106:1971
5473:1976

41st Precinct
(Hunts Point)

Source: New York City Police Department, *Statistical Report:*
Complaint and Arrests, 1971–1976.

ened the residential commitment of middle-class inhabitants, many of them Irish and living in single-family homes. They moved rapidly across Fordham Road into Kingsbridge and Mosholu. This, according to Ed Korn, was their third or fourth change of address since World War II. It started twenty-five years ago, when the Irish fled 135th Street in the South Bronx for the areas around 175th Street. A few years later they moved to University Heights, and now have moved again. Their children still return to the University Heights area to attend parochial schools such as the parish school of St. Nicholas of Tolentine Church. Today, however, the church has only a fragment of the 20,000 parishioners which once made it a powerful force in the borough.

For its part, Co-op City helped to drain Jewish residents out of the central portion of the Grand Concourse, creating vacancies and a resulting weakening of the housing market. Once flight starts, rents tend to soften. "The landlords have a problem with vacancies," says Korn. "They look for people, but the problem is there are no middle class replacements moving in. So to reduce their vacancy rates the landlords find they must rent out to poorer tenants."

The best guess is that some 10,000 moved out of the Concourse area below Fordham Road to Co-op City. The irony now is that Co-op City seems to be affected by the same forces that played upon the Concourse. According to a well-placed official at Co-op City, in 1977 there were 750 vacancies out of 15,000 apartments in the high rises. The problem, he says, is not one of finding applicants; it is one of finding *white* applicants. All those who applied for the apartments were black or Puerto Rican.

As it is balanced now, 30 percent of Co-op City's apartments are rented to minority group members, and 70 percent are rented to whites. Fearing that an increase in minority tenants would begin to "tip" Co-op City, the tenants' council, which includes both white and minority members, decided to hold the 750 apartments vacant until it could find more white tenants. The cost of the forced vacancy rate is approximately $2 million a year.

While the Irish gave way on the west side and the Jews in the center, over on the east side, in the neighborhood straddling Belmont Avenue near the Bronx Zoo, the Italians seem to have had more staying power. But while older people are willing to stay, younger ones are beginning to move out, many of them to Yonkers. They still come back on Sunday morning to attend services at Our Lady of Mt. Carmel Church and to visit parents and grandparents.

* * *

When the lights went out in the Bronx, it should have been no surprise that the bulk of the looting would happen in the neighborhoods recently occupied by the poor. Of the 473 stores looted in the Bronx, 277, or 58 percent, were situated above the Cross Bronx Expressway, outside of the South Bronx. As noted in Chapter II, the looting was particularly heavy on Tremont Avenue (58 stores), Burnside Avenue (43 stores), and the Grand Concourse just south of Fordham Road (54 stores). Those three avenues alone accounted for one-third of all the looted stores in the Bronx.

The fact that the bulk of the looting occurred in the Central Bronx that night does not mean there are no poor people left in the South Bronx. It means simply that unlike the central part of the borough, the commercial life in the South Bronx has deteriorated to the point at which there is little left to steal.

Immediately below Fordham Road, the Upper Concourse runs like a solitary commercial strand, with dozens of deteriorating tenements crowding in on it from the side streets that parallel and run into it. Walking these streets in a cold November drizzle, we saw dozens of young men gathering in hallways or converging at street corners. In July the people who live in these buildings poured out into the Concourse in waves. One Puerto Rican merchant who protected his sporting goods store with a shotgun, backed up by several armed friends, told us that the crowd extended from one side of the Concourse to the other, across six lanes and two dividers.

Another Concourse merchant said again and again that "you cannot comprehend how many people were out there . . . *everyone* was out there."

As on Flatbush Avenue in Brooklyn, the deterioration in the blocks on either side of the Grand Concourse just below Fordham Road is remarkable because of its recent vintage. Alec Zander, 40, whose large furniture store on the Grand Concourse was cleaned out that night, grew up in the Concourse area and always saw the Avenue as representing a nearly unattainable social height. "My goal in life as a kid was to live on the Grand Concourse," said Zander, whose mother worked two jobs to support him and his brother. "It was the epitome of arriving. If you dated a girl from the Grand Concourse, that was money."

He was at home in Rockland County on the night of the blackout, when looters tore open his scissor gates and poured into his store. Not only was his showroom cleaned out, but so was the basement which he said contained forty bedroom sets, each consisting of a bed, dresser, chest of drawers and bedside table. So much furniture was looted from his store and from others that night that Zander attributes the 50 percent post-looting fall-off in business to competition from stolen merchandise sold on the black market.

Zander and his partner said they reached the store at about midnight; each was armed with a shotgun. "I was running into the street grabbing people like a crazy person," says Zander. "If my partner hadn't prevented me, I would have shot someone."

Like many people who rise from humble beginnings, Zander looks back at the hard times of his youth as generating a sense of morality and a stoical spirit, the absence of which he sees as a basic cause of the looting. "When I was playing stickball as a kid and the cop told you to move, you tasted his billy club if you didn't move," he said. "Now, of course, it's a very liberal society. It was just too easy for the looting to happen. What's to stop it from happening next time?"

While it would seem to require a considerable effort in the direction of optimism, one person, at least, thinks the South

Bronx is on the brink of a great leap forward. There it is, says James Marley, director of the North Bronx Family Service Center; the land is all cleared, good transportation is available to Manhattan and the rest of the country, and there is plenty of available labor—the perfect combination for industrial development. "The problem before was seen always as the people and all the crime," he said. "Well now, the people are all gone and so is the crime. I think the South Bronx is on the verge of a big boom."

Flatbush

That some eighty stores were hit in Flatbush shocked many New Yorkers who still pictured the area as a bastion of middle-class Brooklyn. Much of it, of course, still is, from the stately, rambling Victorian houses on the blocks south of Prospect Park to the tidy brick and stucco domiciles closer to Kings Highway to the south.

But severe deterioration has spread into the northeastern section of the community. Some forty-nine stores were looted on Flatbush Avenue itself, many of these in the strip from Parkside Avenue to Albermarle Road, where most of the changes have occurred. In the last few years the poor have been crossing the one-time barrier of Flatbush Avenue and moving onto blocks toward the west.

First to feel the influx have been the schools. P.S. 152 on East 23rd Street and Glenwood Road, for instance, which seven years ago was two-thirds white/one-third minority, is now the other way around. The same is true for P.S. 139 on Cortelyou Road. Working and middle-class people, many of them older, have been vacating the three- and four-story walkups in the Parade Grounds area below Prospect Park, and even down some of Ocean Avenue itself, long a Jewish middle-class stronghold. As in the Bronx, no replacements for these middle-class people exist except for the poor, who themselves are fleeing from decrepit sections of Brownsville and Bushwick. "You're living in Brownsville, and you've got no heat or hot water and someone tells you there's good apartments in Flatbush, so you move," one staff member of the city's Office of Neighborhood Stabilization said.

As is the case in the Bronx, the change usually begins once vacancies occur; landlords inevitably get desperate for tenants. "What usually happens," says Ira Harkavy, chairman of the Community Planning Board in Flatbush, "is the top floor of a four-story walkup becomes vacant, and because that's the least rentable apartment, the landlord can't find middle-class people to take it, so he rents to a poor family. Maybe they bring in children who are disruptive, and gradually the building clears out and fills up with welfare people."

The susceptibility of an area to deterioration seems to depend on the nature of its housing. The area west of Ocean Avenue, for instance, from Church to Foster Avenues, is filled with large, gracious one-family houses built in the early 1900s rather than the three- and four-story walkups one finds to the east. Here, there is strong evidence of a small immigration of young middle-class families. Some of them teach at Brooklyn College nearby; some are disappointed "brownstoners" who cannot afford houses in Park Slope, across Prospect Park, but still want a house in the city. In 1978 the houses were featured in a spread in *New York Magazine*.

The stores on Flatbush Avenue itself, however, seem to be following a pattern similar to that of the Upper West Side of Manhattan in the nineties and hundreds. Older, more conventional, largely Jewish-owned stores are gradually giving way to small Korean markets and cheap variety stores whose owners put tables out on the sidewalk, piled high with two-dollar sneakers. Rents along the avenue are down from the $1,500 level of eight or nine years ago to $600 a month now, says Harkavy, "if you can find a tenant." A severe blow to Flatbush Avenue came in 1970, with the opening of the huge Kings Plaza Shopping Center at the southern end of Flatbush Avenue near the middle- and upper-middle-income neighborhood of Mill Basin. "Why shop here, when you can go there, park your car without any trouble and go to a better class of store?'' Harkavy asked.

Street crime on Flatbush Avenue is on everyone's mind, and on many days the female decoy team from the 67th Precinct can make five arrests for purse snatching. But reliable statistics are difficult to find, since the areas abutting the avenue are served by three different precincts. The 67th Precinct, which made 142 arrests the night of the looting, reports that the crime rate, after going up in 1975 and 1976, went down in 1977. Purse snatchings were off by 16 percent last year.

In November 1975, the city set up an Office of Neighborhood Stabilization in Flatbush to try to organize community groups in order to stem their panic. It also helped organize a Flatbush Avenue Task Force, which succeeded in making facade improvements on one commercial block. Overall, however, the effort is on a small scale.

"During the looting Mayor Beame went to Brownsville, which is already all gone," complained Pamela O'Shaunnessy, a reporter for *Flatbush Life*, one of three community newspapers published by the Courier Life Company, which itself is moving its office from Flatbush to Sheepshead Bay. "Why didn't he come here, where there's still something left? Do we have to wait until Flatbush looks like the South Bronx?"

X

THE OLDER POOR NEIGHBORHOODS

The traditional poor communities were also looted that night. In some cases the looting was worse, in some it was as bad, and in others, less than in the transitional areas. In several instances the extent of looting on the commercial streets seemed to depend as much on accidental factors as on sociological ones. In the Jamaica section of Queens, the fact that no more than thirty-one stores were looted all along Jamaica Avenue was partly because the large public housing projects south of the avenue are effectively walled off from the strip by the Long Island Railroad yards, which are difficult to traverse. Another reason for so little looting was that the police in Queens, many of whom live near the 103rd Precinct and could respond quickly, made more arrests earlier in the evening than in any other borough. This warned would-be looters that they would face consequences from their acts.

But again, and it bears repeating, those unguarded stores

containing food, clothing or sellable goods, which were situated in neighborhoods occupied by the poor, whether in an old established ghetto or a transitional neighborhood, were looted that night.

Harlem

The initial Planning Department statistics suggested that Harlem was not looted heavily during the night of the blackout. And because the community suffered little fire damage and merchants tended to replace their broken windows promptly, a tour through the area a week and a half after the blackout only confirmed the statistical impression that things were cooler there than elsewhere.

Subsequent investigation shows that this was not the case. In the first place, the Planning Department list did not include stores on the police list, which eventually increased the total for all of Manhattan by nearly 50 percent. In Harlem, as it turned out, from 110th Street to 151st Street, running roughly from Fifth Avenue to the Hudson River, a total of 76 stores were looted, which places the community in about the middle range for that night.

Secondly, Harlem had some extra help on hand when the lights went out. This played a crucial role in the 28th Precinct's defense of the community. Since November of 1976, the precinct had been host to a special Tactical Patrol Unit working as an antidrug force on nineteen heavy narcotic blocks from 110th to 120th Streets. Consisting of 56 police officers and 3 sergeants, the unit was on duty when the blackout struck, and served to triple the number of men the precinct had on hand to thwart the initial thrusts into stores. What is more, the TPU was deployed as a single unit along 125th Street, the main commercial artery of Harlem, which accounted in large part for the fact that only 16 stores were looted there that night. Indeed, of the 42 stores struck within the precinct's boundaries, 28 hits were on streets other than 125th. "The way the crowds were that night," said Lt. Matthews, "if they saw you making a lot of arrests on one block along 125th Street, they just didn't go to another block, they got off the street entirely and went somewhere else."

Bedford-Stuyvesant

In the mid-1960s when the antipoverty programs were first being organized, few ghetto communities seemed quite so ready to benefit as directly as Bed-Stuy. For one thing, many of its approximately 400,000 residents were already middle-class homeowners, and it had a vast network of block associations which not only gave people a sense of identity but provided the organizational structure to get things accomplished. In addition, the community's housing stock generally consisted not of the rundown tenements of Harlem or the Bronx, but of some of the soundest, finest-looking brownstones in the city.

Since the 1960s, few minority communities have been provided with so much money and attention from government agencies, foundations and political action groups. These efforts have also resulted in substantial private investments. The area is home to the Bedford-Stuyvesant Restoration Corporation, one of the most respected and successful revitalization projects in the country. Leaving aside the feelings of hope and heightened community spirit created by Restoration, the corporation has poured a considerable amount of money and resources into the community since its founding in 1967. As of December 1977, 1,123 individuals had been given home mortgages valued at $22,895,996; 126 businesses had been financed to the tune of $19,873,762. Of the 11,085 people seeking jobs, the corporation had found work for 8,282. Its exterior renovation program had spruced up 3,682 houses on 106 different blocks, and employed 4,015 people for at least

half a year. Some 342 additional units of housing had been renovated, with 230 more in progress, and 457 units had been
newly constructed.[1]

In addition to Restoration, Bed-Stuy has the Youth in Action Community Corporation which, with its fifty centers, is
the largest antipoverty program in the entire country. Then
there is federal housing money, which has resulted in more
federally subsidized housing than in any comparable area.

Along with attracting money, the community has generat-
ed an impressive degree of political power. As senior black
assemblyman in the state legislature, Thomas Fortune of Bed-
Stuy chairs a number of powerful committees. Bed-Stuy's
state senator, Vander Beatty, ranks second in seniority
among black senators, and serves as assistant minority leader.
The area's congresswoman, Rep. Shirley Chisholm, was the
first black woman elected to the House, and regularly gets
high marks from fellow legislators for her effectiveness in
committee work.

Of course, as was the case with most antipoverty efforts of
the 1960s and 1970s—and there is no reason to think it was
dramatically different in Bed-Stuy—the prime beneficiaries
tended not to be the people closest to the bottom, but those
up-and-comers who had clout enough in the community to direct the benefits their way. This area still had its share of
unemployed youth, poor schools and general poverty, all of
which became even more severe in the 1970s because of inflation.

Nonetheless, and taking it all together, it seems that if
there was any neighborhood during the night of the blackout
whose inhabitants could have been restrained from looting because they had a sense of pride and a stake in their community, it would have been Bed-Stuy. And initially it looked as if
considerable restraint was indeed shown. Early Planning Department reports put the number of stores looted there at only
60, far fewer than in tiny Crown Heights, and even fewer than
on the Upper West Side of Manhattan. One of the area's commercial hubs, Fulton Street and Nostrand Avenue, suffered
only 3 or 4 looted stores. Also, officials of the Restoration

Corporation reported that there was little trouble in areas adjacent to its complex. This was echoed by newspaper editorials in Boston and Philadelphia; those observers saw the relative calm in Bed-Stuy as the one "bright spot" in the blackout.[2] They interpreted it as evidence that revitalization efforts can indeed pay off in time of social disturbances.

A closer examination of the looting in Bed-Stuy, however, gives a much different picture. From talking to merchants, police, antipoverty workers, looters, eyewitnesses and planning officials, we found that while the looting there was not as destructive as on Broadway in Bushwick and in some other areas, Bed-Stuy was looted as extensively as most poor neighborhoods in the city. The total number of stores hit was not 60, as originally reported, but 139, or about 20 percent of the borough's total. The discrepancy in numbers stems from the fact that because of time pressure, the initial Planning Department report did not include survey data from one of the two community planning boards in Bed-Stuy. In addition, it failed to include stores on the Police Department list which Planning Department researchers missed in their automobile survey. Even the revised figure of 139 stores fails really to reflect the total participation of Bed-Stuy residents that night, because it does not take into account the stores looted along Broadway in Bushwick; this is the dividing line between the two neighborhoods. Of the 140 arrests for looting on Broadway made by the 81st and 83rd Precincts, 56, or 40 percent, gave addresses in Bed-Stuy.

Looking at a looting chart of Bed-Stuy, it seems evident that wherever poor people lived near unguarded stores containing desirable merchandise, the stores were looted. As they did elsewhere, the hours of darkness held out the brief chance for people to provide themselves with direct, personal, material benefits—indeed, benefits that came in a more direct material way than could be furnished by the most imaginative antipoverty program. The hope that somehow poor people would forego such an unexpected opportunity because of an ideal—be it community attachment, respect for private property or a feeling of gratitude for the things that are done to ease their plight—was not sustained by the events in Bed-Stuy that night.

According to the combined reports from the planning and police departments, every significant commercial block was hit. To the north, 49 stores were looted along Dekalb Avenue; to the east, 8 were struck on Reid Avenue as far as Atlantic Avenue; 40 more were hit on and off Utica Avenue from Atlantic Avenue to Eastern Parkway. Twenty-seven stores were looted on Nostrand between Fulton Street and Eastern Parkway. Four more were struck on side streets and 11 on Fulton Street between Franklin and Throop Avenues.[3]

While the looting was general, two questions remain. Why were only a handful of stores looted near the commercial hub of Bed-Stuy, at the corner of Fulton Street and Nostrand Avenue? And what happened to the shops in and around the elaborate Restoration Corporation complex at 1368 Fulton Street?

Fulton Street at Nostrand Avenue is the border between two Bed-Stuy police precincts, the 79th and the 77th; it is also a substation for the Transit Authority Police. By all accounts the police arrived at the junction early in the evening and stayed there in force all during the night. In addition, many storeowners in the area stay open until late at night, so they were just closing their doors when the lights went out, which provided at least some deterrent to looters.

According to Albert Telemons, owner of a jewelry store on the northwest corner of Fulton and Nostrand, who was just closing up at 9:30 that night, it was only two or three minutes into the blackout when gangs of people struck the Maurice Stewart Fine Furniture store at 1213 Fulton Street. Shortly thereafter, within fifteen minutes, Telemons guesses, eighteen to twenty police arrived in six cars, with three or four men to a car. From then on, he said, police presence at the corner was constant, and it was augmented by cars patrolling up and down the two cross streets. "Every time you'd look," he said, "there'd be police cars going up and down Fulton Street."

The comparatively large number of police in the area resulted in an unusually high number of early arrests in the vicinity of the junction, which acted as another deterrent to heavy looting.

Of the 117 arrested by the 79th Precinct, 14 were picked up at the Fulton/Nostrand corner, more than at any other corner in Bed-Stuy. Within a block of the corner, a total of 28 were arrested, nearly a quarter of the precinct's total arrests. While citywide, the police made only 7 percent of their arrests before 12:30 A.M., during the first three hours of looting, the 79th Precinct pulled in 55 percent of its Bedford/Fulton/Nostrand arrests during that time. And it made most of these arrests (53 percent) in the first hour and a half.

Further east along Fulton Street, where the police line started to thin out, store owners got help from other sources. One of them was the Dagger Investigative Services, Inc., which regularly guards the Restoration Corporation complex of stores. Consisting of fifteen to twenty Suni Muslims from a nearby mosque, the organization is unorthodox in its methods but extremely formidable and effective. Its Chief is Richard Darden, 34, a former personal aide to the late Sen. Robert F. Kennedy and a private investigator who worked as an undercover agent for the Knapp Commission during its investigation of police corruption in 1972. In 1975 Darden, who is black, convinced Restoration to discard the traditionally geriatric rent-a-cops it was using as security for its store complex and give his then-budding outfit a try. Through his chief aide, Hussein, who was recently decorated by the city for successfully evacuating hostages in a robbery incident at John and Al's Sporting Goods store in Williamsburg, Darden hired unemployed members of the mosque at $2.50 an hour and began training them in Kung Fu and other manly arts, "not so much for defense, as for discipline," he said. He chose Muslims, he said, because he thought people with "some other incentive would be more likely to show up regularly for work."

As uniforms, Darden designed a quasi-military get-up consisting of purple berets, blue blouses and pants, and jump boots. His men are also equipped with walkie-talkies, truncheons and, for "psychological reasons," fairly long daggers carried in sheaths on their belts. The uniform and the men's training in the martial arts are designed to present an aggressive facade intended to discourage trouble before it starts.

"Most ex-policemen in security work believe in apprehension," says Darden, a low-key and self-possessed man and a weapons enthusiast who carries a Walther .380 PPK under his dashiki. "My approach, however, is deterrence." Whereas guards at the stores in downtown Brooklyn tend merely to chase shoplifters out of the store, Darden's men run after them for four or five blocks, and catch them, too. Young males wandering aimlessly around the complex are stopped and politely but sternly asked their business. "I wanted the word to get out that we didn't tolerate that bullshit anymore. We want them to know they can't come here and steal like at other places."

Darden has unquestionably succeeded in scaring off many undesirables, and also in establishing a fairly wide reputation for his men in the community at large; but his organization has been criticized for rousting innocent people along with the troublemakers. Some community people question whether his tough tactics are always necessary.

Morale among the Dagger employees is extremely high. While the normal complement at night is only seven men, during the night of the looting, eight others arrived voluntarily from as far away as Queens, to help out. From Darden's own account and the accounts of his men and other witnesses as to what went on at Restoration at different times during the night, the extra men found they had plenty to do.

Architecturally Restoration's $2 million complex was designed, at least partially, with security in mind, and it doesn't offer much of a target during any kind of social disruption. Its shops are all located on an inside gallery with no display windows fronting directly on the street. Pulldown gates cover the Fulton Street entrance, where most of the crowds were that night. The entrance to the east was blocked by a deep excavation for a new Pathmark store. Only the back was open to potential looters, and that fronts on a well-kept low-income housing project on Herkimer Street built by Restoration itself.

Even so, the looters came very close. Directly across the street, they smashed the window of the Apollo Formal Wear Store and made off with what the owner said was about one-third of his rental tuxedoes before Darden's men chased them away. Across Throop Street, east of Restoration, looters rammed a dumpster through the iron sheathing of the Discount Liquors at 254 Throop Street, and stole what the owner said was $40,000 worth of recently delivered liquor and wine.

In front of Restoration, several groups of young men would come up from Nostrand Avenue, look at the broken window at the Apollo, eye the guards and the Dagger van with its dome light, and then move on. At least once by Darden's account, and twice by the account of one of his men, a group of young men made a frontal assault on the Fulton Street gates by jumping on them and trying to pull them down. By then Darden's men were equipped with riot sticks—five-foot, oak coal-shovel handles—and used them to drive the attackers off.

It is Darden's opinion that his men made the difference that night in terms of whether Restoration would be looted. Had his men not been there, he said, "I think the place would have been destroyed." Captain Sullivan at the 77th Precinct, which has Restoration in its territory, agrees with Darden's assessment. When the lights went out, Captain Sullivan had only twenty-four men stretched out over the whole precinct. "We had a choice," he said. "We could have held maybe two blocks with those men and let the rest of the precinct go, or we could spread out and do the best we could with what we had. Restoration had the manpower, so what they did was just hold their own block."

For two or three blocks east on Fulton Street, stores were not so lucky. A liquor store on Throop Street north of Fulton was not touched, but the owner said friends came down when the lights went out and protected it for him. In the next block going east on Fulton, Jack's Bargain Store lost twenty thousand dollars' worth of clothing when looters broke in through the back. In the next block, at the Fulton Pawn Brokers, 1543 Fulton Street, looters used a bumper jack to pry up the gates at about 10:30 P.M.; they stole twenty thousand dollars' worth of merchandise. Diagonally across the street, the Associated Foods store lost four thousand dollars' worth of food when looters came in through the roof, as they have done twice more since the night of the blackout, despite the presence of three German Shepherds. "Look," said the owner philosophically, "when they want to come in, they come in. The dogs don't stop them." Normally he keeps a light on in the store, because two years ago burglars burned his store down by mistake, he thinks, when they dropped a candle they were using to light their way.

In the other direction on Fulton Street, from the Restoration complex to Nostrand Avenue, there are not many of the kind of stores that were looted that night. And every unguarded store that did have desirable goods *was* looted. Of the two "lootable" stores in the first block, the Apollo tuxedo store was saved only after Dagger guards drove off looters, and the other, a new record shop, was not in business that night. The other shops were not the kind generally hit during the blackout: a Chinese restaurant, a small market, a beauty aid store, a dairy store, a pizzeria, a meat market and a travel agency. On the south side of Fulton are a used furniture shop, a beauty parlor, and a store that sells religious articles; none of these were attractive to looters.

Looters had better pickings further up Fulton Street toward Nostrand Avenue, where Restoration guards had little effect. But here another kind of security force took up the baton. According to all accounts, this part of Fulton was saved in considerable part by five Arab brothers who own the Pioneer food store on Fulton, halfway between New York and Nostrand Avenues. Shortly after the lights went out, they arrived in two cars and patrolled both sides of the street, armed with shotguns and clubs. Among the store owners who felt the brothers made the difference that night was Stanley Moel, owner of Moel Hardware at 1316 Fulton Street. "I'm glad

Restoration's here," he said. "They're good for business, good for the area. But I don't think it made any difference for us that night. We were helped by the Arabs at Pioneer."

The Arabs also kept an eye on the It-Fits Boutique across the street from Pioneer, as well as on the F & L Men's Shop and Burdel's TV Center. "Two, three stores, they tried to break in, and we beat them," said one of the brothers, who declined to give his name. "When they see the shotguns, they run."

"They were riding their cars up and down the sidewalk, swinging bats and waving their shotguns," said Sol Cohen, whose furniture store at 1292 Fulton Street is several doors down from Pioneer. Looters broke into the front part of the store and made off with some television sets and other appliances before an employee showed up. He was helped by the Arabs to drive the looters off. "I give them a lot of credit," said Cohen, echoing a general sentiment in the ghetto that the wave of Arabs who are moving in and buying up stores in poor neighborhoods do not lie down so easily before criminals. "They don't care who you are; they don't take nonsense from anyone."

* * *

As in other neighborhoods, the streets in Bed-Stuy may have seemed alive with people, but only a small fraction of the community's population was involved in either the looting or the watching. In the residential blocks between Fulton Street and Myrtle Avenue, people reacted to the blackout as they did anywhere else in the city: after their initial nervousness vanished, they sat on their stoops, drank beer and generally enjoyed the strange experience.

Mrs. Johnsye Williams moved to her house at 521 Putnam Avenue, in the geographic heart of Bed-Stuy, shortly after her wedding day in the middle of the Depression. Now sixty-seven and a widow, she is a lively, active lady despite her use of a walker. Mrs. Williams was raised in Newport-News, Virginia, the daughter of a real-estate entrepreneur who was also involved in the city's first black bank. Her father managed to send all his eight children to college. Mrs. Williams, whose brother is a lawyer and Recorder of Deeds in Washington, D.C., was attending Hampton Institute when she came North on what she thought was merely a visit. Instead she met Mr. Williams, then a student at New York University who was working part time as a mail sorter in the U. S. Post Office. Shortly thereafter the couple was married; Mrs. Williams never went back to Hampton Institute.

The Williams's bought their three-story brick row house—one of sixty on the block—for $500 from an Italian family, as the neighborhood was beginning to change color. (By the end of World War II, the Italians, Irish and Jews had left, and the block was all black.) After his graduation, her husband could find no other work, so he stayed on as a clerk at the post office until his retirement several years before his death in 1970. The couple's four children have all shown the results of close and careful nurturing.

One daughter, who has her Master's degree from the Bank Street College of Education, teaches in an experimental school in Bed-Stuy; another graduated from the University of Maryland and is a retired Army colonel; a third is married to a master sergeant, a recruiting officer at Fort Hamilton. Her son, who is currently taking business courses at New York Community College, runs a driving school in Flatbush and owns three rental properties there.

Mrs. Williams now lives alone on the first two floors of the house; she usually rents out the third floor for $200 a month. Two or three times a week she calls for a car and visits friends, with whom she plays bridge. She is also actively involved in functions at St. Augustin's Episcopal Church, which is housed in the former Catholic Church of the Nativity on Classon Avenue at Madison Street. Despite what seems to be her fairly comfortable existence, Mrs. Williams is constantly urged by her children to move out of Bed-Stuy. "My children want me to move somewhere else," she says. "Live with them. They'll buy me a co-op, a condominium, anything. Well, I have no intention of moving. I've lived here forty

years and this is my home. 'Mama,' they say, 'you've lived
there long enough; come live with us.' 'No,' I say, 'I'm
here!'"

One thing keeping Mrs. Williams on Putnam Avenue is
that for the past eight years she has been the very active president of the local block association. Formed twenty-five years
ago, the association holds a nearly constant round of cake
sales, raffles and block parties to raise money for beautifica-
tion and security measures, including tree planters, tree
guards to keep dogs away, and chain link fences in back yards
to discourage burglars. It also acts as a sort of godparent to
the block's children. Every summer the association gives a
large party and dispenses school supplies such as notebooks
and pencil boxes. "We feel that if we take care of the children, then it makes them more conscious of the block," she
said. "It's theirs and they help keep it nice."

The Restoration Corporation has proved helpful in several
ways. Not only does the association take children from the
block ice skating and to the movies at the complex, but it uses
the Billie Holiday Theatre there for fund raising. It recently
raised $500 in a theatre benefit held in conjunction with the
Daughters of the Eastern Star. The association also bought its
exterior gas lamps through Restoration. While it had to pay
list price, it saved by paying no sales tax.

As with other neighborhoods in Bed-Stuy, Mrs. Williams's
block must constantly take action to fend off crime and deterioration. Within the block the population tends to be fairly stable and hold strictly to middle-class values. But the apartment
houses on the large crosstown avenues house more crime-
prone groups such as drug addicts, unattached, unemployed
males and alcoholic derelicts. An abandoned building that is
ignored, a rooming house allowed to deteriorate, can provide
a beachhead for trouble.

Consequently Mrs. Williams and the thirty-five or so members of the association worry constantly about housing conditions. One house, number 517, was abandoned several doors
away, and the block spent a solid year tracking down the owner and getting the city to close it up. "We had to get it closed

up before the derelicts got it," said Mrs. Williams. Rooming houses on the block are also a sign of impending deterioration because they invite single men and women whose concern for the community is not high. At present two rooming houses exist on the block, and Mrs. Williams's group is forever badgering the landlord to have them painted and to get rid of loud noisemakers. "In one of them they would have parties all night, with the windows open, no screens, no blinds," she said. In another instance, a single male roomer brought three cars onto the block which were alternately in and out of repair. "He was the sweetest thing you'd want to meet," she said, "but he'd go off for days and just leave the cars there, and we couldn't get the street swept properly."

Crime comes in spurts, and usually residents know where to look for the culprits. Last spring the block was hit by a series of burglaries which people felt were performed by the boyfriend of a girl living in one of the rooming houses. "We threatened the landlord to close him down unless he kicked the couple out," Mrs. Williams said.

Some problems even the block association is powerless to combat. One of these is the idle young men lounging up on the avenue at Throop Street. They harrass people going to and from work via the IND subway, which stops on Fulton Street. "They just stand around like flies," Mrs. Williams said, "You have to walk right through them while they make remarks. It's awful."

Thinking of the loungers makes Mrs. Williams muse about the way people in general seem to have lost self-respect in recent years. "In the Depression, people had no money certainly, but they sold apples, collected rags, anything. At least they sold something and didn't ask for anything." Mrs. Williams has no objections to welfare for people who really need help. Indeed, many families on the block are on relief, although Mrs. Williams doesn't know exactly how many because it's not something people generally want known, she says. But she cannot abide welfare cheating, nor such aberrances as drug addiction. "I'd say 50 percent of the drug addicts know what they're getting into," she says. "I think they should all be put off on an island."

The night of the blackout, Mrs. Williams was visiting friends in Flatbush, but arrived back on the block by 10 P.M. With the gas lamps lit, the block wasn't as dark as most, and people sat on their stoops talking until late in the evening. Twice her son and daughters came by to check on her, but the night went quietly by. The only effect looters had on that part of Putnam Avenue was that they came on the block to sell stolen goods.

"We saw this woman, and I don't know how her conscience would let her do it, but she was wheeling a baby carriage full of stolen things down the sidewalk to the corner at Throop. There her boyfriend helped her get it all in a building on the avenue. It's one thing to steal something, but then to just walk down the street parading it in a baby carriage! People I talked to were perfectly disgusted. They said they wouldn't buy a thing."

The whole episode of the looting, in fact, appalled her. "I think a lot of it was just mass hysteria. Someone started it, and it was just follow-the-leader after that. And you know what I think? I think a lot of them felt that 'I'm due this' and 'Let the city pay for it.' They are the same kind of people who go on relief and feel the world owes them something. They're people with a grudge."

Even now Mrs. Williams feels if bad times appeared again, she could find some work to get her by. "Even at my age and with all my difficulties, I would get something. It probably wouldn't be just what I wanted, but I could get something." While she and her husband never considered themselves poor, she went to work as a clerk in Family Court to help put the children through school, and there were always things she wanted but could not afford.

"For instance, I don't have a fine home—I mean, a really fine home," she said matter-of-factly. "If we hadn't done all we had to send the children to college and all, I could have had a nicer place to live. But I'm not sorry, and I don't believe my children owe me anything but respect. I don't feel they owe me anything but respect—for me and for themselves.''

* * *

While Mrs. Williams refuses to leave Bed-Stuy because it is so involved with her past, other black people—mostly younger, middle-class couples—have begun moving back to the community because they see hope for its future. One of these couples is Wilbert and Brenda Fryson, who bought a brownstone at 63 Chauncey Street, four blocks east of the Restoration complex, in the fall of 1975.

Mr. Fryson, thirty-eight, is a chunky, muscular, energetic man who was born in Orlando, Florida, and works as a supervisor in the Bureau of Location and Support of the Department of Social Services. His office looks for absent fathers of welfare families. Brenda Fryson is thirty-seven, the daughter of a bus driver. She was raised in a brownstone in the Fort Greene section of Brooklyn. She works as a career counselor at the Manpower Development and Training Program of the Board of Education, which is about a ten-minute walk from her house. The couple met at St. Paul's College in Lawrenceville, Virginia, where Mr. Fryson had gone to play basketball and Mrs. Fryson was sent because her parents wanted her to have the experience of going away to school. After getting married in 1964, the couple lived in an apartment in Clinton Hill until they moved to Bed-Stuy.

With a combined income of $34,000, the Frysons could live in any number of middle-class neighborhoods in and outside the city, including Laurelton, Queens, an integrated community which is home for many middle-class blacks. They chose to come to Bed-Stuy for a number of reasons.

For one thing, it is close to both their jobs, and transportation is available to almost anywhere. Nearby, the Fulton Street bus goes to downtown Brooklyn; the Utica Avenue bus goes to the Kings Plaza shopping center, and the IND "A" train takes them quickly into Manhattan. For another, Mrs.

Fryson had a special interest in seeing that her seven-year-old daughter grew up in an area where she could make lifelong friends, something Mrs. Fryson felt deprived of in her own childhood. "For me, it was difficult making the lasting relationships that I would have liked to have," she said. "All through school, I went to schools that were mostly white, and after school we all went our own way. I would like it to be different for her."

Then, too, the couple was intrigued with the idea of owning and renovating a brownstone, but found that houses in such traditional brownstone sections as Fort Greene, Park Slope and Clinton Hill were too expensive. "We'd read all the stories about people doing brownstones on the West Side and on the East Side," said Mr. Fryson, a softball addict who in warm weather plays for no fewer than seven different teams. "Brenda would go on the house tours, and we had friends doing it. Then when I saw David's house, I was sold." David is David Danois, an architect who at one time worked for the Restoration Corporation. His brownstone on Marcus Street in Bed-Stuy includes a cathedral ceiling stretching clear to the skylight in the roof, a feature he helped the Frysons incorporate into their own renovation plans.

The house they eventually found is a three-story brownstone built in 1901 and located just across from Fulton Park, a tiny triangular strip of green filled with maple and chestnut trees and surrounded by a wrought-iron fence. The house cost $25,000. While the couple made a good combined salary, they had little capital, and so needed a sizeable mortgage. First they tried their savings bank, Metropolitan Savings, which agreed to lend them money, but with penalty points. The monthly payments would have totaled $400. Through a friend at Restoration, the couple secured a $23,990 mortgage from Banker's Trust without having to pay any point charges. Then, for renovation work, the couple found they could get a loan of no more than $5,000 from Chemical Bank or $7,000 from Citibank. Again a friend at Restoration placed a phone call to the Office of Urban Affairs at Chemical Bank, which agreed to raise its loan offer to $10,000, the minimum the Frysons needed to begin redoing their house. The renovations have been in progress for more than two years and are now about two-thirds done. Mr. Fryson has done the rough work and some carpentry, such as exposing brick walls and building platform beds and furniture. Help was needed in installing new wiring and plumbing and in the construction of two new bathrooms and a new kitchen. Mr. Fryson has plans for a bar and recreation room in the basement. "He says he won't let me go down there," said his wife, "but that's what *he* thinks." When completed, the renovations will eventually run to about $20,000.

Besides working on their house, the Frysons are deeply involved in the local schools. Mrs. Fryson is secretary of the PTA for P.S. 262 in District 16, on Macon Street, where her daughter attends classes. She considers the schools as *the* struggle in the community, and while she and her neighbors appear to be winning the battle, it is a long, hard fight. One problem is the school's reading level: it is high for the district, about average for the city, but low when compared to the national norm. In the last two years the parents at P.S. 262 have dug into their own pockets for about six hundred dollars' worth of reading machines and software to help the children learn.

Another concern of the PTA is that none of the teachers live in the community, and most are reluctant to become involved in anything that is not strictly classroom work. "One reason we don't get quality education here is the teachers are so afraid," said Mrs. Fryson. "We've got teachers who are scared to death of second-grade students. They're scared of black people; they're scared to get off the subway, scared to walk down the street, scared to stay at night to attend our meetings." She said the PTA has tried to get teachers to come to meetings with parents "so we can get some input from them and to let them know the parents are interested in their children and interested in what's going on in the classroom." Aside from the school's principal and assistant principal, however, the only staff members who attend are the para-professionals who live in the community, she said.

The problem of crime is on people's minds, the Frysons said, but not to the extent that nonresidents might think. "We know it's there, and we do the things we have to, to protect ourselves because we live in the inner city," said Mrs. Fryson. She and her husband plan to buy a burglar alarm system when they can afford it; their block association is talking with the police about setting up a blockwatching program to help cut down on a rash of recent car thefts (Mr. Fryson's much-prized 1968 Stingray was stolen in 1977). Also people are concerned about a group of twelve- and fourteen-year-olds who hang out at the local subway stop, harrassing passersby and now and then snatching a purse. Mrs. Fryson's sister had her own purse stolen not long ago, and although she gave the two culprits "a merry chase," said Mrs. Fryson, she never caught them.

While people are naturally anxious about crime, it doesn't dominate their lives. "We don't think about it to the point that we're afraid to go out," she said. Much of their comfort comes from the block itself, whose residents make a point of looking out for each other. "Nobody could go into a house on this block and drive off with all your furniture without anybody doing something about it," she said. "And that's what it's all about, really. I feel comfortable here. You're not afraid to let your children go out and play. There's always someone watching. It's a real community feeling."

The Frysons also feel warmly toward the Restoration Corporation. "It's such a vast pool of resources, and they've done such a fantastic job for the area," Mrs. Fryson said. "The thing that Restoration has really added is something you can't touch. It's more the spirit of the thing. What they've done is to rehabilitate the spirit of the community."

The night of the blackout was hot, and as is usual in the summer, Mr. Fryson was out playing softball in St. John's Park. When the lights died, he made his way home to his wife and daughter, and the family spent the evening talking with neighbors and drinking beer on the stoop. None of the looting touched the block directly. From her work with young people in the schools, Mrs. Fryson thinks that much of the stealing stemmed from deep-down hatred. "I may be wrong," she said, "but I think a lot of it was not really because they wanted the stuff; it was a way of getting back at someone who has his foot on their head. I feel like it myself sometimes, the way you walk into some stores and they treat you sometimes like you're dirt."

She said that in her conversations with young people she sees a lot of hatred lying not far below the surface.

I think it's more intense than it used to be but it's gone underground, which is more dangerous. It frightens *me*, even. We were told when we were growing up how to survive, but not to hate. But in these youngsters coming up, you hear a lot of 'I hate white people. I hate whitey.' They've got no skills; they can't read or write; they don't know how to do anything. All they know how to do is hate.

Her words were spoken not out of contempt, but compassion.

Lower East Side

Of all the neighborhoods looted on the night of the blackout, the Lower East Side was the only one we found of which it could be said that there exists a genuine community spirit which may have helped to keep the stealing to a minimum. This is particularly true of the northern part of the neighborhood, between Houston to 14th Streets, where only eleven stores were damaged. Some of the forbearance, no doubt, was due to the paucity of stores that sell expensive, attractive merchandise along Avenues B, C, and D. But from interviews and discussions with the police, it seems that the lack of looting was due just as much to the fact that although Type I and Type II looters were on the scene in reasonable numbers, those of the Type III group, the more stable members of the poor community, tended to stay home. In fact, they acted much as New Yorkers did during the 1965 blackout: they turned it into a festival.

Jesus Laviera, assistant director of the Association of Community Organizations, went around organizing bonfires. Portable radios blasted out rock music for dancing, and residents had beer fests supported by kitties of spontaneously donated dollar bills. In an event which underscores the cultural diversity and extremes that exist in New York City, some of the residents even sacrificed an animal—namely, a cat—to ward off worse disasters than a mere blackout. "Without the looting," said Laviera, "other aspects of the blackout are a lot of fun, like a feast."

Some leaders patrolled what they consider the parameters of their community, from 14th to Houston Streets, and went immediately to protect vulnerable businesses whose owners they felt had dealt squarely with the residents. Bonds between poor people and shopkeepers, surely extraordinary in urban life, seemed to be taken for granted by the people we talked to. According to Laviera, "candles and batteries did not go up in price—here they were the same price they sold for everyday." When favored stores were looted, many people in the community expressed genuine sadness. For instance, Bernie Goldfield's tiny clothing store on East 9th Street, near Avenue D, has catered to residents for more than for thirty years.

When Bernie's was looted shortly after midnight that night, the scene was watched by a bright ten-year-old named Eddy Garcia who lives across the street from the shop, between Avenues C and D, in a second floor apartment. It was a horrifying experience for Eddy, although he has unquestionably seen his share of violence and shocking behavior. (It was in this area that we witnessed a man openly shooting up in the doorway of an abandoned building around 10:00 o'clock one morning.) Bernie meant something special to Eddy. As the looters began to attack the store, Eddy actually got involved and telephoned the police. He also took his long, heavy-duty flashlight and shined it on the looters. The police made several sorties into the area and eventually arrested three people, but before the night was over, the store was invaded and cleaned out. We asked Eddy how he felt when he saw the looting, and he said, "I laughed," attempting to mask his true feelings about the incident. Faith Wright, who runs a school lunch program on the bottom floor of a neighborhood building and had already heard Eddy's story, asked in surprise, "You laughed, Eddy?" Eddy then lowered his head and replied, "No, I cried."

Just why the Lower East Side, or at least the northern part of it, experienced less looting that night is open to speculation. For one thing, as noted by Bertram Beck, director of the Community Service Society and formerly head of the venerable Henry Street Settlement House, the community has had a tradition of social service institutions that were in existence long before the Puerto Ricans arrived. Programs to organize the poor begun by Mobilization for Youth and other groups laid some of the structural and ideological foundation for the national antipoverty programs.

The community has also had a tradition of grass-roots political organization. And its hard-fought battle with the United Federation of Teachers over control of the local school board—a struggle it lost in the end—used community chauvinism as a basic organizing tool. Artie Santiago, a thirty-four-year-old Democratic district leader and director of a local antipoverty organization, said that shortly after the lights went out he went out on the street to "talk quickly and quietly with the young people."

A panic began quickly. I heard shots while still in my apartment. When I got out, crowds had already gathered. We started rapping about the fact that a lot of people were doing a lot of work to rebuild the neighborhood. We talked about the fact that we've been through the riots and all we got out of it was a devastated neighborhood. The people settled down. The rioting was contained very well. . . .

The rioting was not a protest, just a bunch of clowns taking advantage of a situation to benefit themselves. The looting was inexcusable. If the social problems are bad enough, you don't need to have the lights go out to rebel. When you're hungry, you're hungry.

We can't afford these kinds of riots anymore. There's nothing left here. The economy is no longer in the neighborhood. We've helped destroy our own neighborhoods in past riots. I know because I've been in them. . . .

You have to understand the panic and understand the hustlers. The junkie population depends on the crowd. They go inside the crowd to do their thing. They egg on the crowd. We had to disperse the crowd before the junkies got it going.

Santiago described his own background as that of a revolutionary activist of the late sixties and early seventies who has joined the political process "to embarrass concessions out of it."

"I represent folks who live in a garbage can. I still believe no concessions are made without confrontation. I just don't believe burning and looting our own neighborhoods produces anything." In normal times Santiago would be the first activist down at the police precinct to protest any arrest in his community. But his feelings toward the looting arrestees were different, he said: "I didn't give a shit about those who were arrested that night."

* * *

The spirit shown by people who live in the rundown blocks on the Lower East Side is such that it catches visitors by surprise. Mrs. Damaris Torres, a mother with several children, has lived there for thirty years, most recently in the Jacob Riis Houses that overlook the East River. "I love it here," she said. "All my friends are here. This is my home. I will never leave Avenue D."

xi

LOOTING THEORY

Many people reacted to the blackout looting as though it represented a new and unique social phenomenon, when in reality it has a long tradition in this country and elsewhere. Looting itself has its origins in military history, in which "invading armies" dressed in uniform have often taken property by force, generally when the rightful owner cannot protect it.[1] Indeed, in the Pacific and other theatres in World War II, many cases exist of U.S. troops looting their own stores under the justification that they deserved more and better food than was alloted to them. In natural disasters and civil disturbances, "invading armies" in civilian clothes plunder property left unguarded when the owner is unable to secure his belongings or the constabulary cannot keep looters from sacking stores and shops at will. The individual who lifted a wounded person's jewelry during the Galveston, Texas, hurricane of 1900, the Vietnam soldier who brought home a painting ripped off the wall of a Saigon home, and the mob that drove away with fifty Pontiacs in the Bronx during the New York City blackout of 1977, all did the same thing: they looted.

Although there are explicit international laws against it, looting in wars and during military occupations has become an accepted custom. When two nations are at war, neither tends to apply its own conventions when dealing with the other, nor is each likely to observe those of the opponent. Within a nation, however, looting in both natural disasters and civil disorders is viewed as an assault on the society's basic mores and values. Inside a society, everyone is expected to live under the same rules of law. In ours the most basic value has been that a person's right to property is sacred. The law, for most of us, is simply that every citizen must earn or pay for whatever he or she gets.

We do tend, of course, to underplay the extent to which property rights and ownership have been abused in our history. They often do not operate in the manner we say they do or in the way we think they ought to. But when looting occurs, these fundamental values are not operating at all, and the public's sense of shock and dismay is understandable. Uncontrolled hordes of people snatching cheap trinkets and expensive appliances as they parade through the streets in full view deals a hard blow to society's moral and ethical gut. Added to the sight of wide-open stealing is often the wanton destruction of property and violence against innocent parties who lose out merely because they happen to own something looters want. But as morally repulsive, socially disruptive and economically costly as looting may be, it has occurred often in our history and in many different places, usually when disasters—such as earthquakes, fires, floods, power failures, blizzards, enemy invasions, police strikes, or civil disorders—cause a breakdown in law enforcement.[2]

The following, for example, is excerpted from the work of Dynes and Quarantelli:

After the Galveston hurricane of 1900, published accounts told of people being summarily shot when they were caught with pocketsful of severed fingers with rings on them. In 1906, after the San Francisco earthquake and fire, the Los Angeles Times reported that 'looting by fiends incarnate made a hell broth of the center of the ruined district.' Sixteen looters were shot out of hand on April 19, while robbing the dead. In his reconstruction of events after the earthquake, reporter Q. A. Bronson . . . noted reports of . . . looters shot in their tracks by Federal troops, miscreants hanged in public squares, and ghouls found cutting off the fingers and ears of corpses for rings and earrings attached.[3]

While such barbarous looting has apparently vanished, looting itself has continued right up to our most recent history. Drawing on Irving Bernstein's classic studies of strife in the Depression, Frances Fox Piven and Richard Cloward point out that "one of the earliest expressions" of unrest among the unemployed was the rise of mob looting."[4] Much of the looting that occurred in this period was not widely known, they say, because "the press refrained from reporting these events for fear of creating a contagion." In New York bands of thirty or forty men regularly descended upon markets. In March of 1930, 1,100 men waiting on a Salvation Army bread line in New York City mobbed two trucks delivering baked goods to a nearby hotel. In Henryetta, Oklahoma, 300 jobless marched on storekeepers to demand food, and threatened to use force if necessary. Bernstein concludes that in the early years of the Depression "organized looting of food was a nation-wide phenomenon."[5]

After the Depression, labor violence and strife over economic conditions subsided. Except for a number of sporadic racial disturbances during the World War II years in Detroit and Harlem, where looting did occur, it was not until the mid-1960s that massive violence and looting became frequent.

Dynes and Quarantelli, in studies of the riots of the 1960s, found that looters come from all segments of the population, females as well as males, older adults as well as youngsters, middle-class as well as lower-class persons. Other research into major urban disturbances of the 1960s suggests that as many as one-fifth of ghetto residents may participate in rioting, and a majority of them, in some form of looting. The McCone Commission found that 600 stores were looted or burned in the Watts disturbances. During the Newark riot nearly 7,000 people were involved, according to a Kerner Commission study, and about 1,300 people were arrested, mostly for taking goods. In the Detroit eruption it was estimated that almost 17,000 people participated; 2,700 stores were vandalized and ransacked. This contrasts sharply with natural disasters, when looting often does not occur at all, and if it does take place, apparently involves a handful of individuals from the general population. For example, during the unusually heavy snowstorms in the Northeast during the winter of 1978, looting occurred in poor sections of Boston, Massachusetts, and Providence, Rhode Island, but did not involve large numbers of people.

* * *

That looting has occurred so often and in so many places does not make it easier to explain than any other form of collective violence. Indeed, theories of scholars on the subject and opinions of lay observers are equally abundant and inconclusive. After they have all been studied, one is still left with several questions: Who loots? Why? Are the looters poor citizens trying to gain material goods they cannot afford, or are they criminals or persons lacking in morality or proper upbringing who steal at any opportunity when risks are diminished?

In academic circles, the view that urban violence and looting have their roots in poverty is consistent with Relative Deprivation theory, or "RD", which holds that violence results from a perception of the discrepancy between what people believe they are rightfully entitled to and what they think they are capable of getting. The emphasis here is on the *perception* of deprivation: how people perceive their relative position in terms of where they are vis-à-vis others, and where they expect to be. People maÿ *feel* deprived even though an objective observer might not consider them to be in need. Conversely the existence of what the observer judges to be abject poverty, or "absolute deprivation," is not necessarily thought to be unjust or harmful by those who experience it.

According to Ted Robert Gurr, author of *Why Men Rebel*, there are three types of deprivation: Decremental RD, Aspirational RD and Progressive RD. A number of well-known theorists have attributed political violence wholly or in part to decremental deprivation.[7] The revolutions that Aristotle held to be characteristic of democracies and oligarchies were said to result from deprivations of this type. According to Pirim A. Sorokin (*The Sociology of Revolution*), the immediate cause of revolution "is always the growth of 'repression' of the main instincts of the majority of society, and the impossibility of obtaining for those instincts the necessary minimum of satisfaction." Marx and Engels argued that the growth of profound dissatisfactions in the proletariat as a consequence of absolute deprivations or oppressions was inevitable, for the worker's pride was destroyed through his subjection to the machine and the market. Natural disasters in traditional societies often gave rise to collective violence, according to Norman Cohn's study of violent millenarianism in medieval Europe.[9] And E.J. Hobsbawn argued that the phenomenon of banditry was most pervasive in the precapitalist peasant societies of Southern Europe "when their traditional equilibrium [was] upset, during and after periods of abnormal hardship. . . ."[10] The late Senator Hubert Humphrey was in this camp in the late 1960s when he said after the explosions in Newark and Detroit, "If I lived in the ghetto, I would riot, too." And Gurr writes, ". . . decremental RD has probably been a more common source of collective violence than any other pattern of RD. . . . Men are likely to be more intensively angered when they lose what they have than when they lose hope of attaining of what they do not yet have."[11]

Those who experienced aspirational RD are angered because they have no way of attaining new or intensified expectations. In the 1960s, for instance, when black Americans demanded more social equality than they had had in the 1940s, "there appeared a shift from faintly held aspirations for equality to an intensely held belief that equality was deserved at the moment."[12]

Progressive deprivation occurs when a prolonged period of objective economic and social development is followed by a short period of sharp reversal. Davies has proposed a model of progressive RD, and refers to it as the "J-curve" hypothesis, which he argues explains the urban rebellions of the 1960s. The period of violence in the 1960s, according to his thesis, occurred after a spell of good times among blacks, followed by a shift to bad times. The income of blacks relative to whites of comparable education increased rapidly towards equality between 1940 and the early 1950s, but then began to decline. By 1960, half the relative gains of the earlier period were lost. Diminishing capabilities, evident in politicians' reluctance to extend political rights and in irremediable economic decline, provided the background conditions necessary for the outbreak of violence.[13]

The deprivation theory has some obvious weaknesses: is there not enough constant deprivation to have violence all the time? Are not many groups—Indians, whites, Chicanos—similarly deprived, but not engaged in violence? When there is violence in the ghetto, the majority of residents, as was certainly the case during the blackout looting, do not participate. Why are some violent and others not? Grimshaw has suggested that since there is always enough intense deprivation to cause violence, the key issue is external control, mainly involving the role of police and agents of authority.[14] And Stanley Lieberson and Arnold Silverman, after studying urban violence in 78 cities, found no support for the contention that riots are a consequence of income gaps between blacks and whites, or that unemployment is a direct factor.[15] Gurr himself has recently suggested that the worst-off are not necessarily the most prone to violence. Individuals in the middle range of the ghetto population, he now says, appear to have higher expectations than those of the extremes: the most poor and the better off.[16]

The U.S. Commission on Civil Disorders (the Kerner Report) concluded in 1968 that the riots of the 1960s occurred because of the "explosive mixture which had been accumulating in our cities since the end of World War II."[17] Also blamed were "discrimination and segregation in employment, education and housing . . . which exclude Negroes from the benefits of economic progress." All resulted in disappointment, a climate of violence, the frustrations of powerlessness, and alienation and hostility toward institutions of law and government.[18]

* * *

The counterpoint to the role of relative deprivation in precipitating violence, is the riff-raff theory, which has three distinct, although closely related, themes: first, that only an infinitesimal fraction of the black population actively participates in civil disturbances; second, that looters and rioters, far from being representative of the ghetto community, are principally the riff-raff—the unattached, juvenile, unskilled, unemployed, uprooted, criminal—together with outside agitators; and third, that the overwhelming majority of the ghetto population—the law-abiding and respectable 98 or 99 percent who did not join in—unequivocally are opposed to and deplore violence and looting.[11]

One of the major proponents of the riff-raff theory has been Edward C. Banfield, a Harvard University professor of government who stirred considerable debate and controversy with his arguments that the urban crisis was primarily the result of the liberal imagination. Banfield saw the violence in cities as a result either of the youthful desire to engage in excitement or the penchant for thieves simply to steal. He writes: ". . . race (and, incidentally, poverty as well) was not the cause of any of the major Negro riots and . . . it had little to do with many of the lesser ones." Urban riots, he concludes, are not so much rebellions as outbreaks of animal spirits and of stealing by slum dwellers.[20]

The Kerner Report, however, presented a thorough refu-

tation of the riff-raff theory. Based on several research studies, analysis of the arrest data and impressionistic accounts,
the report concluded that the rioters were a "small but significant minority of the Negro population, fairly representative
of the ghetto residents, and especially of the young adult
males, and tacitly supported by at least a large minority of the
black community."[21]

The riff-raff theory may have its detractors among some
scholars; it is nonetheless strongly supported by others, and it
remains widely held by the general public. In the aftermath of
the blackout, it was perhaps the major reason advanced by
most people for the looting. Indeed, *The New York Times/*
CBS poll mentioned earlier is a strong indication that most
New Yorkers, across all groups, agreed with the basic view of
the riff-raff theory—"that violence is caused by "those who
steal if they think they can get away with it." Indeed, the
statement that received the highest negative rating in the poll
was that the looters were "poor and needy." It was rejected
by a margin of 74 percent to 18 percent.

xii

CONCLUSIONS

Those who joined the public debate over the causes of the looting generally divided themselves into two rival camps. On one side were the looters' advocates, who claimed that residents of the neighborhoods where the outbreaks occurred were poor, deprived citizens who rebelled against their desperate circumstances. In support of this view, a *New York Times* editorial called the looters ". . . victims of economic and social forces. . . ." Professor Herbert Gutman of the City University of New York wrote in a *Times* Op-Ed essay that the looters' behavior was similar to that of the Jewish women in the Kosher Riots of 1902.[1] Even President Jimmy Carter joined the controversy and told the nation that it was important to recognize that the looters were hungry, although he was careful to include a condemnation of the violence.

On the other side, the major view was that the looters were

simply thieves. Diane Ravitch, a professor at Columbia University's Teachers College, wrote in another Op-Ed Page piece: "There is a vast distinction between action undertaken by those prepared to take the consequences of their actions and the pillaging of those who rob their neighbors, destroy local business, and stockpile the booty for resale."[2] The writer Midge Decter, in an article in *Commentary*, a journal basically sympathetic toward civil rights and black advancement in the 1960s, constructed her own variation on the *Daily News* view of the looting as a "night of the animals."

". . . to anyone watching them at work, surging out of the shadows in a horde and scurrying back into the cover of darkness as the police cars came by," wrote Decter, "the imagery suggested is one taken from insect life—from urban insect life—rather than from the jungle or forest."[3]

It is important to recognize that to choose a theory is to choose a policy. As Henry Bienen has aptly pointed out ". . . if one chooses to focus on conditions, it follows that massive attacks on the economic and social order are called for. . . . If one chooses to emphasize the precipitants of violence and to see criminality pure and simple, calls for law enforcement are in order."[4] But while this kind of polarized view of mass violence has been the standard way of evaluating its causes, our view of the blackout looting is not as clear-cut.

First, although criminals played an important initiating role at the onset of the disturbances, it is too simplistic to call the looters riff-raff. First, it would ignore the enormous differences among the looters which we have attempted to show in the earlier profiles. Moreover the impact of the social and economic system in producing crime has been recognized for almost two decades. To ignore the linkage would set us back even more in our response to the social problems that still linger in urban areas. The argument of critics like Decter, who questioned whether the looters really wanted jobs in the first place, fails to account for the clamorous appearance after the looting by thousands of black and Puerto Rican teenagers who jammed manpower centers to apply for work in the blackout cleanup, work that paid only $2.35 an hour for no more than 25 hours of work a week. In their studies of the reaction to the 1960s riots, Michael Lipsky and David Olsen wrote that labeling the rioters as riff-raff was part of an attempt to dismiss the people attacking the social fabric as those who were undeserving.[5] As they suggest, much of the commentary in the aftermath of the blackout aimed to avoid any serious consideration of grievances, and lumped all the looters together as "criminals."

In our view, the main cause of the violence was the serious national economic decline that has created exceedingly high levels of unemployment and high prices for food and other necessary goods, and has substantially worsened the living standards of the poor. Prices of food, clothing and rent, as measured by the Consumer Price Index, rose 86 percent from 1967 to 1977. In 1977, the welfare allotment for a family of four in New York City was $129 every two weeks, a rent allowance of up to $218 a month plus food stamps. These figures were based on a standard of need stabilized in 1974. Added to inflation, the national unemployment rate for blacks in general doubled over the past ten-year period, from 7 percent to 14 percent. As a result, unemployment in minority areas of the cities has skyrocketed. Businesses and manufacturers continue to leave the city; since 1969 the jobs lost amount to 650,000. In addition, in 1977 the city's Department of Employment estimated black teenage unemployment at almost 70 percent, and Hispanic unemployment at nearly 80 percent. The people arrested that night had unemployment rates far above those who were arrested during the 1960 riots: in some cases they were almost *three times* as high!

But while the looters suffered inordinately high rates of unemployment, to call them "hungry" does not accurately describe the nature of their plight. Surely they were not hungry in the sense that peasants were in the French Revolution, when hunger denoted being without food and bread. In a welfare state where basic subsistence is provided to almost everyone, widespread hunger in the literal sense is no longer the issue. What the looting did seem to say was that the issue is a more general, spiritual kind of hunger, deeply felt by citizens of the ghetto because they simply lack the goods, the material things, and the power to consume what is so thoroughly emphasized by the media in our society. In other words, the welfare check or the unemployment allotment is important for survival, but just surviving is not enough in a society that is constantly beating into the minds of all its citizens that all kinds of goods and luxuries are necessary for a decent life. Indeed, to have those things is the way to participate in the American Way of Life.

There are other messages we think were transmitted that night. The looting manifested drastic shifts in the location of poverty, and its growing complexity. The Harlems, Bed-Stuys, Brownsvilles and South Bronxes remain, but poverty is now widely dispersed to neighborhoods not even yet known to the public as areas under stress.

Another important change in the inner city is that within the traditional ghettos and in some outlying areas as well, there has developed a corps of hardened, street-type urban dwellers who operate in a shadow economy of hustle and crime. They are mainly men, first cast off by the working of the economic system, then frequently asocialized in youth homes and prisons, from which they bring a rather fierce and brutal institutional culture to the streets, and finally ostracized by residents of the ghetto themselves. These men are virtually unreachable by conventional social programs or general economic improvement. The Reverend Clarence Norman of the First Baptist Church in Brooklyn said, "Unless we find a way to reach them, any effort at revitalization in the ghetto is in jeopardy."

Adding to the complexity of urban poverty in New York is the arrival of new immigrant families, many of them illegal aliens from Latin America and the West Indies. The suggested participation of large groups of West Indians and Dominicans in the blackout looting indicates that the historic characteristic patterns, particularly among West Indians, of strong family structure, thrift, and belief in advancement can no longer be expected. The reasons for this are not clear, but it is possible that poorer people from more rural areas are now coming to New York from the West Indies, and find it extremely difficult to fit legitimately into today's tight urban economy.

Finally, although we reject the riff-raff view and have strongly emphasized economic forces instead, we do not rule out the importance of cultural, psychological and moral factors. Indeed one of the deeper meanings of the looting is the additional support it provides for the notion that the poor have less awe for the institutions of society than outsiders think they do. The basic arrangement between society and the individual—the social contract—which calls for the individual to accept certain rules and obligations in return for society's protection and guarantees, has worn extremely thin among the poor in general, and for those in Stage I and Stage II, it seems to have broken down completely. What is more, the fact that the contract is so little honored by other segments of the society, most notably by business and government elites whose penchant for cheating and criminality has been widely reported in the media the last ten years, makes it easy for ghetto dwellers to discount any call for restraint and forbearance on their part as exceedingly hypocritical.

In sum, our argument is that the looting was the result of a variety of forces and attitudes which included declining legitimacy, criminality, and material aspirations accented by the media. But the root of it all, the fundamental source, was the poverty and growing hardship both in old ghettos and in neighborhoods more recently inhabited by the city's poor. The looting did not take place in the context of the kind of social upheaval that occurred in the 1960s, and, therefore, unlike the previous decade, there was no articulate cry for power or advancement uttered prior to the blackout. In that sense the looters were indeed not conscious dissidents. To say they were simply hoodlums, however, ignores the social and economic realities of urban life which became startlingly visible in the darkness of the night of July 13, 1977.

APPENDIX

The following interviews were done by Douglas Williams, a thirty-three-year-old political science student in the General Studies program at Brooklyn College. Williams lives in a poor community, and he had a rapport with the looters that we, as outsiders, found hard to achieve.

The first interview is with John Davis, a twenty-one-year-old unemployed veteran who lives with his mother and siblings in Brooklyn. The second interview is with Cindy Robinson, a seventeen-year-old mother attending high school in the Bronx. She is supported by welfare and lives with her mother, who is also on welfare.

Undoubtedly the reader will question some claims made by the two interviewees, as do we. The major benefit of the statements comes from the looters' observations of the blackout and their comments about their own lives and values.

We caution readers not to take any sentence or paragraph in isolation, for the meaning of the ambivalences, contradictions and obvious exaggerations would be lost.

Some details concerning personal description have been disguised to protect the identity of the individuals.

I: Interviewer   *J:* John

I: How about your schooling?

J: All right. I got a diploma, an equivalency diploma. I went to high school for a few years and I dropped out in the eleventh grade. 'Cause, you know, I got a athletic scholarship. Yeah, I got a lot of offers from, like, Grambling. To play football. But I blew the scholarship. They told me I had to go to junior college first, so I said the hell with it, I'll just quit school—so it was my fault. It was all my fault. I didn't go to class. I did it all wrong. About seventeen, I quit. I wish I would still be in school now. If I could change with the way things are right now.

I: What were you doing after you left school?

J: I joined the Marine Corps. I did four and a half years in there. I just got out in April.

I: How did you end up there?

J: I don't know how I did it. I had to be crazy, really. I signed that piece of paper.

I: I knew guys that signed up, man. I knew guys that were on leave and the next day . . .

J: Yeah; I know a lot of guys that did. I asked for it, though. I signed that piece of paper and I was gonna do. I said let me do all or nothing.

I: Yeah, you gotta give yourself a positive attitude.

J: Yeah. I had a positive attitude in the beginning. I forgot to tell you. I was on unemployment during the summer, you know. I was on unemployment for the whole summer but it just wan't enough money. You know you can't live on unemployment.

I: So when did you get out?

J: I got out on April 15, 1977. No shit. I just got out. It'll take a while, you know. I ain't got readjusted yet. I'm startin' to. To get money in my pocket and get out and get it on.

I: Where were you born?

J: Right here; Brooklyn, New York, Kings County Hospital.

I: And your mother?

J: Well, my mother was born in New York and my father was born in Alabama, in Birmingham, Alabama.

I: Where's he now? Where's your father?

J: Where's he now? He's in Birmingham.

I: Did you ever get in trouble with the law?

J: Yeah; when I was seventeen I got busted.

I: So what did you do after you got out?

J: Gone on unemployment, got used to being on the street again, being back in New York. When the blackout came I was getting unemployment. I started working on the fifteenth. Anybody come out with an honorable discharge can go on unemployment. We were playing ball, playin' basketball. And when the lights went out, everybody started screamin', you know. At first I thought it was just the project lights and I started looking around; everywhere I looked the lights were out. Everybody started yelling and, you know, like mass confusion. Nobody knew what to do. I heard someone say, let's get Pitkin Avenue.

I: That's what they said?

J: Yeah. Let's get Pitkin Avenue.

I: To do what? What were you gonna do on Pitkin Avenue?

J: To loot. At first really I was yelling just to be fancy, yeah, yeah, yeah, yeah. I didn't do anything, man. Everybody on the block was out. Everybody was going down Pitkin Avenue. People from all over was down there. Everybody just walkin' and talkin'. We went down to this gift shop and they just started getting shit and then they broke. We broke into the stereo shop, getting stereos and what not. You get whatever you can carry, whatever you could carry. The first trip we didn't have any plan or nothing. The second time we tried to get everything home. That's when the police started coming. The first time I couldn't carry all the stuff. Everybody got something. Everybody got a stereo. People that had no jobs standing around said, I'm going to Pitkin Avenue, see what I can get, but I came home with the stuff, brought it to my room. My mother was outside. She asked me, where did you get it from? I said, Pitkin Avenue. I guess, you know, she figures I'm grown; she can't tell me to stop; she can just tell me, be careful and what not. Don't get caught. I hadn't even thought about getting caught. You know, I felt good that I got over it. Police came and everybody in the whole world was there tryin' to get people off the street, but there wasn't enough po-

lice. The people just moved to the other end. Everybody was comin'
out of the jewelry store with gold and diamonds and rings and what
not, stuffing it into their pockets. I didn't see anybody get busted on
Pitkin Avenue. There were too many people. They were just trying
to move them away. Yeah, this is the second trip, they weren't after
nobody. This was an opportunity, you know; I mean, the lights went
off. I mean, you never know. And like, there were people trying,
watching traffic and helping people and what not, and the dude stand
right next to him got shot. That's when I decided to come home. I
had a stereo in my hand and I said, let me get my own ass the hell out
of here 'cause they just started shooting and they didn't stop. Bang,
bang, bang, bang. The dude went down. So I said, I'm going home.
And I couldn't find nobody or nothin'. I couldn't find anyone. I just
went the hell home. I wasn't gonna get shot. I was comin' home
down Eastern Parkway with the stereo, and someone behind a tree
with a pipe or somethin' hit me with it. I don't know what he was
trying to do, but I dropped the stereo and ran. I said, fuck it; let me
get out of here.

I: So he got the stereo.

J: I don't know. I guess he did. I didn't stop and look . . . Is-
raelis or Arabs—yeah, Arabs—something like that, that owned the
store, they started shootin' people, started shootin' into the crowd,
right? I know about four people that got shot right here on the corner. They just started shootin' and everything. I know this lady that
got shot real bad. They just started shootin'. Yeah, everybody was
lootin', everybody went out. And so, like, we all ran back here to
the building. We all came back to the building and what not, and
then we went back outside and we started up the block again . . .

I: O.K., so now the last point you talked about is that you came
right down, right?

J: Right.

I: So I'm gonna ask you the same thing again. The first time you
went up to Pitkin Avenue what did you do?

J: Right. Excited, excitement you know; I was up. I was
charged, you know, with the excitement of the moment. The lights
was out, you know; we was gonna see what we can do. Like, I was
really charged up—

I: O.K.; so the second time?

J: The second time it was about the same thing. But, like, the
second time I had thought more about what I wanted to get, you

know. I was bent on making some cash, you know. That's what my mind was working on, get all you can, you know. Nobody knew what time the lights was coming on or nothing.

I: Get wise and get those goods?

J: Right. Get the most expensive things you could get your hands on before the lights come back on 'cause we knew it wouldn't be too long.

I: What did you think about? Were you gonna sell it or were you gonna keep it?

J: I was thinkin' along the lines of selling. Selling, definitely.

I: You wanted cash?

J: Right. I wanted money. That's why most of everything I got is sold.

I: And you weren't worried about selling it. You knew the people was gonna buy it.

J: Right. I knew it. You got anything to sell cheaper than in the stores, you gonna find a buyer. You got people out here selling thirty-dollar sneakers for ten dollars. You gonna tell me people aren't gonna buy thirty-dollar sneakers for ten dollars? Everybody would. You know, I'm saying you out here sellin' hundred dollar medallions for twenty-five dollars. Gold medallions and what not. You know, definitely.

I: O.K.; so the third time you went back to Pitkin Avenue and nothing was going on.

J: Nothing was going on. The police was down there. I didn't want to get busted. So I said, let's go on up to Utica.

I: O.K. You got to Utica, right, the first time. What was the feeling?

J: I mean we just was walking up there, talking. When we got up to the corner we saw how everyone was breaking up Utica Avenue. We just jumped into the mood, you know? Like they said, when you're Roman, do what the Romans do. We just went crazy.

I: Second time?

J: It was like the same thing, you know.

I: Third time, after L.D. got busted?

J: After L.D. got busted, that's when I started thinking.

I: But you was still going?

J: I was still going but I was thinking: damn, it's time to get whatever else I want so I could get the hell out of here. I was plannin' on moving and like—

I: Yeah, but that's the same time that you went into the clothing store so you got what you wanted. At that time did you know that L.D. got hurt?

J: I didn't know that L.D. got caught. I didn't find out till the next day that he got caught. L.D. got caught on the third trip. I didn't know what trip he got caught on.

I: O.K. Now, so we're dealing with the fourth trip; two guys shot him.

J: Yeah; that's when I said it's time to go home.

I: And you started to head home. And as you headed home you got hit.

J: Right. I got hit in the arm, my shoulder.

I: O.K. What did you feel then?

J: Fear. Fear. I had one thing in mind. Get to my house as quick as possible. And I ran into a brother on my way home and we came around here and they were all startin' to break in, so we said, let's see what's happenin', so we went in there; we said, let's go see what's happenin' in there. So we went and started walkin' up the block, you know. We was walkin' up the block. By the time we got to the corner, guys that owned the store, they pulled up and started busting caps on the corner at the store. And we turned, backed around and ran back into the building, right? And they left. So we started walkin' back up the block, mainly to see if anyone got shot or what not, you know; to see if anyone was layin' out there 'cause we got a lot of friends that we knew was out there and were concerned about my friends. I wasn't thinking about taking nothing. I was worried about if my little brother was in the house or what not, and what was doing on the corner, but when we started walkin' that way they had started shooting up that building. That's when I came in the house to stay. I said, the hell with it; I'm goin' in my house.

I: O.K., so now, like I asked you before: did you have any feelings towards the people who owned the store?

J: You know, I figures the people who owned the store, they wasn't really losing that much.

I: Did you think about that they were white, black, Puerto Rican or whatever?

J: Naw, I wasn't thinking like that.

I: All you were thinking about was yourself?

J: Right. You know, I was just thinking about getting what I can for myself, you know.

I: Because you see that the people were, what?

J: I figures that most of them was white anyway. Most of the people that owned, most of the owners was white. You know, they might have black managers there, but most of the people that owned the stores were white. The way I see it now, at that time I was going around and I didn't think like that, but I sat down and deliberated what went down and who lost what, and I was even thinking about how much was lost, but I also read that they're gonna get it all back. They claim it for their insurance and they claim it back on their income tax as a tax deduction. Everything they lost that they get. And most people, all they had to do was bring in new merchandise and in a couple of days they, you know, after reading the paper I deliberated to see how hurt they really was—

I: A few days after, after reading about it in the newspapers, how did you feel?

J: I feel happy 'cause I got over it and I didn't get busted. I mean, I wouldn't just go out and just start ripping people off like that. But it was an opportunity, you know; it was like a gift. It was like the man upstairs said I'm gonna put out the lights for twenty-four hours and you all go off, you know, and get everything you can. Those who get caught, get caught. Those who don't—well, more power to you. And that's the way it came down, you know. You see, I mean, all the businesses that got torn up, most of them are back in business except for the ones that got burnt down, which was really wrong; but like, people just couldn't, you know, nobody really thought about what they was doing. Everybody was lootin'. A lot of people was just outright—it was fucked up, the way they went about doing what they did, you know. 'Cause everybody could've come off and nobody didn't have to get hurt. If people woulda acted like they had a little bit of sense, act like some kind of self-control.

I: How do you figure they could do that?

J: Some people just don't give a fuck about other people. They don't give a damn. Some people was just out there being destructive. There was people out there just tearing up shit, just to be tearing up. I mean, there were people out there doing it. Just tearin' up. Burning down stores and shit, you know, hurting people purposely. Some people were just out there for that purpose, just to be doin' stupid shit like that.

I: And you don't believe in that?

J: Naw; I mean, I was out there 'cause I'm a poor person and like, you know, lock a hungry dog up with some food, you know he gonna eat it; that's what a poor person is. I mean, when he sees a chance to get what he wants . . .

I: Just let me ask you this, then: why do you consider yourself poor?

J: I am poor. I'm not talkin' about poverty-stricken but I mean—

I: Man, you said here you're poor. Why do you consider yourself poor?

J: 'Cause I can't afford the things I want.

I: That's what you think it is?

J: Right.

I: And when you consider the things that you want—if you can get them, you won't be poor.

J: I'm not poor then. And as far as I'm concerned, I'm talking about me, my own personal self, like, you know, I'm not talking about standards, I'm talkin' about me myself. I can't afford what I want. That's what I went out there and got. The things that I couldn't afford. Not that I really needed these things, it's just the things that I wanted that I couldn't afford.

I: Let me ask you this, then. What do you want?

J: Well, this particular time I went, I wanted those boxes, you know, the music boxes; I wanted sneakers; I wanted the gold, the diamonds and what not; I wanted money in my pocket, and I went out there to get it. You know, it wasn't necessities; it was just things I wanted for myself, you know. I mean, everybody wants a color television, a stereo. . . .

I: Did you get a color TV?

J: Yes, you know.

I: How long did it take to get rid of everything?

J: The day after.

I: The next day?

J: Yeah, the day after. I sold everything. Everything except four color TVs we couldn't get to. 'Cause when we had 'em then, the police had a stake-out.

I: How did you know they had a stake-out?

J: Because somebody spotted them. Somebody that I was down with, when they was going out to check out the stuff, they saw the stake-out, so they came and let us know. They set on us for a while. They set on us for a week or so; they were watching us, waiting for us to go get the stuff, so they could bust us. They know, I don't know how they knew that it was in there.

I: Somebody had to tell them.

J: They might've. A lot of times, like, after the blackout they would go into neighborhoods and into abandoned buildings and check out and what not. They were looking out for shit. Somebody might've told them. They just wanted to bust somebody, I guess. As far as I know they might've checked the stuff out for themselves. You never know what they do. I mean, everybody's a thief. Everybody's got a little dishonesty in them. 'Cause, like, anybody goes in the store, and the guy who owns the store turns around and goes to the back and you're just, like, alone in the store—that's like telling you to take it. I mean, I wouldn't do it.

I: Let me ask you this. What do you think you would do? Let's say this is night time and the light went out again.

J: I don't know. I'm not too sure I'd go back out there again. Now that I know the risk. Like, the first blackout, I was too young to be out on the street, you know, that was about sixty-five—sixty-five or sixty-three? No, sixty-five. I was nine years old, you know; about nine or ten. I was too young to go out on the streets. I was old enough to remember, was old enough to know what was going on, but, like, I was still too young to go out on the street and loot. My mother wasn't gonna let me out of the house.

I: Yeah, but there were little kids out there.

J: Yeah, but my mother wasn't gonna let me out of the house. My uncles was out, you know.

I: Sure; this last one—

J: Yeah, but look how the times are now compared to the way times was in sixty-five. They are much blacker, 'cause right now I got my little brothers and sisters. At their age I didn't even try, I didn't even think about doing those things.

I: Do you think your mother was strict on you?

J: Yeah, she was harder on me than she is on all the younger kids now. But, you know, she was younger and the way the people, the world looked on you was different than the way it looks on you now. People raise children differently in seventy-seven than you did in sixty-five. The people, the country went through a complete change, you know; you got more people in power, you know, moral standards that went lower.

I: You think so?

J: Yes it has, much lower.

I: You think it went lower or it's adjusting to the times?

J: Adjusting to the times. It's adjusting to the times, really. Changing with the times, everybody's saying, you know.

I: Do you think you will ever get married?

J: Yeah. I know I will if I find the right person, but it won't be for a time. See, I'm not financially set for marriage yet. Right now I'm working, trying to make some money. I'm trying to get some grants so I can go to school. If I get this grant I'll be going to law school in Ohio for six years. I'm gonna study corporate law. Because I want to go to school, get a good education or a formal education 'cause I want a good-paying job. In order to get a good-paying job you got to have some kind of formal education, some kind of college degree, and you gotta know: someday I wanna be living in a higher standard of living than what I'm living in now. I wanna be able to give more to my children, give my children more than my parents can do for me. And I feel like I got the opportunity to do this now, so I might as well use it. I'm gonna use every opportunity I can. Anything the man gives me I'm gonna use. So you know education benefits myself.

I: You say you're gonna use anything they give. How do you feel about the blackout? That's an opportunity to use now?

J: That's an opportunity. I was thinkin' about the risks, you know, the blackout. Now I may not be as lucky now that I understand the risks, you know, about what can happen. I don't regret doing what I did; I don't regret it. The only thing I regret about the whole blackout is that so many people got hurt. You know, I mean, a lot of people got hurt stupidly that night and the way people acted, I mean. You know, a lot of people got hurt, but they didn't concentrate on that, they concentrated on the people whose shit got torn up and the people who got arrested. There's plenty of people around here who got hurt. But, you know, I don't really regret what I did, but I'm not sure if I would do it again, and if I did do it again I would go about it a whole different way. I would be systematic. I would have the whole thing planned out.

I: How would you do that?

J: I would know just where I would go to.

I: You would know exactly where you were going.

J: Right. And I would know just what stores to hit too, and I wouldn't go with a whole bunch of people, just me and another couple of guys, and I would try to do it as quietly as possible.

I: Yeah, but I mean, there's gonna be a lot of people out there.

J: Right, but I mean, everybody doesn't got to know what you're doing. See, I mean, you got to figure out what to loot. Most people just stood around and waited for somebody else to do something. Like, they waited for somebody else to hit a store and then they crashed the store, like—they busted into it.

I: So what would you do?

J: While they were crashin' in the store over there I'd be in over here, trying to break in without a whole lot of noise. I can't afford a crowd to watch, to see 'cause now they know who broke into it. I'd try to be the first one in there and get as much as I can and get the fuck on out. So, you know, before everybody got in there. I wouldn't stay probably 'cause I would know what I wanted and, you know, I'd get rid of it quick.

I: How would you do that?

J: I'm not sure. It would depend on the situation, the time, you know, and what I was doing at the time the blackout came.

I: Let's say you were in the same job you are in now.

J: The job I got right now?

I: Yeah. Let's say that you had some money in your pockets, how much money you figure? O.K., let's say you had some money in your pocket, what would you do?

J: I'd probably go out there again. I'd probably go out there again.

I: What kind of money would you need in your pocket to stop you from doing that?

J: Oh, it wouldn't just have to be money. It would have to be my position in life. Like if I was to go to law school, and have a nice paying job, and be established in a firm or something.

I: Before you get there. Let's say you were in law school.

J: And it happened? No, I wouldn't go out there at all. Not at all.

I: Why?

J: Because I wouldn't take the risk of getting busted for lootin' and having to go to jail and blowin' my schooling. It's not worth the risk. You know, if I go to school I could get a job that pays more in a month or just as much in a month, you know, or probably more in a couple of months, than what I made out there doing that, and the risk isn't worth it.

I: How much did you make?

J: I made about two thousand dollars and some change. I mean, it was good for one night; it was good; I got over it. You know, it ain't certain that the next trip I would get over like that.

I: What did you do with the money, spend it?

J: No, banked it. It's in the bank. I'm not crazy. Right now, what I'm doing right now, I'm not sure what I'd do right now. I might try.

I: What are you makin' now?

J: I'm makin' four sixty-seven an hour. If it was now I wouldn't be out there as long as I was. I would just do things systematically for myself and my house. Systematically, and I try my best not to get busted, you know.

I: Did you ever think about a life of crime?

J: A life of crime? Yeah, I thought about it, but it ain't for me.

I: Why not? You thought about how hard it would be?

J: It's not how hard it would be. It's just that that's not the way I wanna live my life. I wanna live my life as a lawyer and spend most of my life in court, you know, in the stands. People always trying to lock me up and what not, I mean, it's too dangerous, dangerous involvement. And the retirement plan, I don't like the retirement plan, you know. The only thing you're guaranteed with a life of crime is your death. I mean, that isn't the kind of life I wanna lead.

I: When you were looting, if you knew the store had a black owner—not a black manager, a black owner—would you still loot it?

J: No, I wouldn't mess it. Yeah, I know a store with a black owner. I didn't mess with it. Nobody did. In fact, those were the only stores that weren't torn up, the ones that the people knew were those with the black owner. Around here? They didn't break into all the stores, just some of them. Just some of them; not all of them. Same thing on Utica; they didn't break into all of them, just some of them.

I: That was the kind of trend then.

J: Yeah; I mean, you look after your people too. Like I said, some people just don't give a fuck and some people care, you know. We had some really stupid guys—the day after the blackout, they came on. When the lights came back on they still carrying on. They still out there doing weird shit. I said, you guys are crazy.

I: Why were so many folks looting?

J: I think that a lot of people who during the blackout went out and stole things was people that don't normally do something like that. Like I said, opportunity arrived. And when people are deprived of something and they see a way to get it, they go out and do it.

I: Can you use yourself as an example?

J: Right. I will use myself as an example, 'cause, like—I mean, somebody come up to me right now and say, let's go break into a store, and I ask them, are they crazy, 'cause, like, really I don't see no sense in that. But I mean, the opportunity arrived, the lights were out, I mean, it was like, it was like a ten percent chance of, you know, really getting caught. It was how fast you moved and how you kept your head about you. That's why I say, you know, I didn't get high or nothing like that all during the night 'cause I wanted my head about me. I stood back and seen, like, I saw people gettin' hurt and people gettin' killed and I said, this is enough, you know; excuse me; I believe all the people that was really out there were the people that normally go out and steal. That was really out there, after that happened. That hadda be people like that. 'Cause, like, most of the people that was really out there during the blackout lootin' and, like, people, you know, like I said, people that work, be people with jobs and workin' and what not, but, like, they see the chance to get things that they, that it would take them years and years to get, so they went out there and did it, you know. You know, when they see people and what not, you know, well, they say, this is enough, you know, you gotta; and everywhere, and the people that went out there the next day, they were just people that normally would steal anyway, you know; they normally do that kind of thing. I didn't 'cause it is the same thing. I mean, if a guy came around here with a truck full of food and he was dumb enough to get out of his truck and go upstairs in the building and leave his truck open—

I: You rip him off?

J: Right. I mean, I will go out there and take it because, I mean, when you come into a neighborhood like that, I mean, this neighborhood around here, you know, I mean, we're not really poor, all that poverty-stricken, but people that lack on a lot of things that they want, that they need really.

I: Why do you say that?

J: A lot of things they need 'cause, like, most of the people in this neighborhood are, like, welfare recipients and what not, people that are not doing too well. This is city housing and what not, I mean, 'cause, like, after all, if my parents didn't have to be around here they wouldn't be here. They would be into a better class of neighborhood where people get more. As you get, you move up in life. When people are deprived of something, if they see what they're deprived of and it's something they need and they've been deprived for so long that they would take it, not because they're thieves, not because they mind working, but self-preservation is the law of nature. And I mean, you see something laying down, the same thing, like, if you was walking down the street and you see a twenty-dollar bill laying in front of the gutter, of course you gonna pick it up, you ain't gonna pick it up and say, anybody lost a twenty-dollar bill? That's the way it work with the blackout man. A lot of people, you know, say, you know, said that, you know . . .

I: You feel the blackout was like a big twenty-dollar bill?

J: Right; that's what it was. It was like a gift, somebody was just saying, when the lights are out y'all just get what you can before the lights come on. I feel the people that really got busted and was out there until four, five o'clock in the morning doing the thing, they had no business out there 'cause when the man started cracking down, people should've had enough sense to realize: well, it's over with now, we had our chance; what we didn't get, we didn't get. The hell with it. You know, you came home, you set back and then you try to rebuild your neighborhood.

I: So you intend to go back to school?

J: Yes; I was supposed to be going back to school in January, but, I was supposed to go to John Jay, but I changed my mind on what I wanted to major in. Like, I was going to major in criminal law and what not and get into the justice department and what not and corrections, but then I changed my mind about that. But now, as I was telling you earlier, I want to study corporate law so I gotta find me another school besides John Jay to go to. So I'm just gonna sit back now and wait, 'cause I don't wanna waste the money I'm getting from the government to go to school. You know, 'cause they gonna pay for my schooling 'cause of the G.I. bill, and I'm gonna wait until I find a school I wanna go to. I hear you, 'cause I got too much I wanna do with my life. You know, 'cause I wanna raise a family, you know, I wanna see my kids one day get my age, right; when they get as old as I am I want my kids to have a whole lot more than I have. My little sisters and brothers, you know, and like, I'm the oldest one here in my mother's house now, and all my little sisters and brothers look up to me and they see what I'm doing. I try to always put an example forward for them, somethin' for them to go for, to shoot for better. I always tell my little brothers and sisters, you know: do better than me. Don't do what I do. I experienced it; I let them know what I got from my experience, see, you know: go on and do better than I am, right; and I don't feel there's no way in the world me goin' to jail or nothin', or getting killed out here in the street. Like, that is no example to have for my younger brothers and sisters. You know, I'm not talkin' about blood; I'm not talkin' about my physical brothers and sisters; I'm talkin' about mentally, as far as black people itself is concerned, like, I'm very concerned the way the world is goin', the way our children is being raised, the things our children are being taught, you know, 'cause, like, all they see— no, all they know is what they see. They never been nowhere else outside of the environment they live in. All they know is what they see goin' on around here. I got a little brother five years old; he be on the street every day and what he sees people do is all he knows, and what he sees me do is what he know, and I feel that by me goin' to jail, doin' a whole lotta time over some bullshit, which is what the blackout was, like, it wasn't necessary for me to do what I did; it wasn't necessary for me to be out there and, like, I'm just glad I had enough sense to see. When the shit was getting to the point where they wasn't plannin' when they had enough of it, well, 'cause I seen. The people down there at City Hall they knew what to do; they knew when the lights went out the poor people was gonna break, get what they can, right; and, like, everybody knew then that the people that owned the stores, they was gonna make theirs back anyway; they wasn't gonna lose nothin'. When they got to the point where they started burning down things, you know, when they got to the point of outright destruction, I mean . . .

I: That's when you felt it was enough?

J: Right. Outright destruction. That's when I started feeling: this is carrying a good thing too far.

I: Did you also feel at that time, 'cause of when the cops started busting heads, when the people started the physical destroying—like burning things and like that. Do you understand what I'm saying?

J: Right.

I: Now you know, like you said, the cops were sitting back doing nothin'—

J: Right.

I: Until what time?

J: Until the people started destroying. I mean, they got to burnin' up things and I mean, the shit really got out of hand.

I: That's when you feel that—

J: That's when I thought it was too much then. I said: well, this is goin' a little bit too far. I mean, everybody should have enough sense to realize that the man is only gonna let us get so much any- way. And, like, the man is saying to me, when he felt we had enough, that's when he came down; but they went to the point of burning down and, I mean, even though we looted these stores as long as we didn't burn up these stores the people was gonna get their insurance money and put stuff right back into these stores. Go out and put the stuff right back into the stores again, put up new windows, and be right back in business the next day. But then they started really hurting themselves when they got to tearin' up and burnin' up these peoples' stores, you know; I mean they got persons tearin' up beyond repair. We was losin' then 'cause that was takin' money out of the neighborhood and stuff like that, you know, and I never would say that we was right for what we did as far as lootin' concerned but, like, people don't think about right or wrong when they got a chance to get what they need . . .

I: O.K. Now let me ask you this: with all the shit that went down, how did your mama feel?

J: My mom? She never really talked about it. I mean, we never really sat down and discussed much, after the blackout. I mean, you know, she knew; she knew what I was doing. She said: just be careful, you know, you could get hurt out there, and then: don't go to jail over nothing stupid, you know. That's what she told all of us, me and my brothers and my friends. She told us, don't get busted, you know. She just said, be careful; don't get hurt. Like, when I came in and I showed her what I got, she said: I know you're not going back outside. I said, no; I'm not going back there, that's for sure. 'Cause she had lots of people from my building in my house, you know, scared to death upstairs. People standing in the hallways, what not. People that live in the next building had a machine gun, you know, and what not. 'Cause I live on the first floor, people sitting out there in the hallway, people lying in the bedroom, the living room, everywhere. The next day me and my brothers we were excortin' ladies back to their house and everything. And the older women they don't have husbands, we went into their house to make sure no one was in their house and stuff like that, you know.

I: So let me ask you this: sometimes the kids are just stealin'—

J: Well, let me tell you this. I can't understand these kids at all. They tear up anything.

I: Do you think the parents have something to do with it?

J: Yes. The parents are off somewhere. You know, I mean, most of the parents, they got older children my age and what not. You know, when the parents get older they can't judge the stuff the way they used to and what not. They got aches and pains, you know; everybody's gettin' old. Like, they don't like to tell you about it, the aches and pains, but they got 'em, you know, and like, they try to feed the children, they try to check 'em, but they can't do it like they used to. And some parents don't really care; that's why they go out and act crazy, you know. A lot of times they just get used to it. They tell you: I don't wanna be bothered with it; the hell with it. A lot of times both parents are working. They have no supervision most of the time. A lot of times parents don't have no time to sit down with them, you know. Shit like that is so hard now. It's really hard to be with them.

I: What does your mama feel about school? You're going to school now.

J: About schooling? No, that's all she does now. She bugs me about schooling. When you gonna start school? When you gonna start school? She definitely wants me to go to school. She doesn't want me to study law; she wants me to finish up in electronics, to go back to electronics. Like, that's what I studied in high school. She feels if I already started like that, why change? Why not go into something I already got a background in?

I: Maybe you'd do better in another thing.

J: I'm doing a lot of thinking about it seriously.

I: Lawyers. They're gonna be a dime a dozen.

J: True.

I: How about your sister?

J: She's graduatin'.

I: From where?

J: I think she graduated; I don't even know which school she graduated from. She graduated from high school.

I: How come she didn't go to college?

J: Couldn't afford it.

I: How about your father?

J: My pop? He graduated from high school. Down south. Yeah, my mother went to school in the city.

I: Where's your father now?

J: I don't know.

I: You don't?

J: Yeah. I ain't see him in a long time I don't know what the hell he's doing.

I: And he graduated from high school?

J: Yeah.

I: What's he doing now?

J: He a cop.

I: He is?

J: Yeah.

I: How long has he been a cop?

J: About eight years.

I: What is his rank; do you know?

J: He's a sergeant. Like I said, I ain't seen him so I don't know what he's doing. So I ain't got, nobody's seen him really.

I: How does your mom get along without him?

J: Ma? She's all right. She definitely all right. Pa? He's all right too, but they just couldn't get along. It ain't my place to get involved. As long as he's not doing nothing to cause bodily harm to my mother, you know, I don't have nothing to say about it, you know. I mean, what can I say? I mean, if I ever get married, me and my wife, you know, we're gonna try telling my children: ain't got no business sticking their noses in. That's for us to say. You know, I don't get involved in their differences at all. Try not to. Unless they come to me. They had their reasons for breaking up; they just couldn't live together really. I rather have seen them break up than live in that storm before they break up.

I: How many brothers and sisters you have? I'm talking about your immediate family.

J: You talkin' about the ones right here? Right here in the house is five boys and four girls. Yeah, it was five and five but my baby sister died in seventy-one. She died, she died of crib death. Two of my sisters don't live here. I know some of them.

I: Some of them?

J: Yeah. I think all together there are about twenty of us.

I: What is it? Half and half?

J: There's nine girls and eleven brothers, something like that. I'm the oldest brother. They're all younger than me. I'm my mom's oldest, yeah.

I: And you're twenty-one?

J: Yeah.

I: How old is the youngest?

J: The youngest one is three. That is, the baby.

I: What message you learned or you think you learned from lootin' that night?

J: From the blackout?

I: Yeah. What do you think you learned from it?

J: Well, I think—let me see. I gotta sit back and really think before I answer. A lot of people react, you know; I feel a lotta people don't use their head. And I learned about myself. I learned that, you know, about myself in general, that, you know, I'm only willing to go to a certain point as far as crime and what not are concerned, and then, you know, I mean really, I learned a lot about myself on that night and a lot about myself on how I feel about people and how I feel about life in general. You know, and it made me think about a lot of things in my life; how, you know, like, next day I sat back and I said to myself: you know, you coulda got killed out there, you coulda been in jail, you know. I really thought, there was a time, you know, that I really think, there was a lot of things that I woulda done against the law that I wouldn't do now all because of what I seen happen in the blackout. You know, and I realize how you can get your, how you can really ruin your whole life, you know, and I learned really that there's a lot of things, I really set back and thought out really how far I wanna go with my life, and I know for a fact now that as far as crime and what not is concerned that is not me at all.

I: Interviewer   *C:* Cindy

I: Well, start on the, when was that? When was it? A Wednesday night or a Thursday night? What night was it?

C: It was July 13 at nine o'clock. A Wednesday.

I: It doesn't matter. Where were you when the lights went out? That's where you start. Where were you when the lights went out?

C: I was home. First we was outside, then we came upstairs and then all of the electricity went off. We was in the living room. And then everybody started going crazy outside.

I: How do you know that?

C: Because we were sitting lookin' out the window. Lookin' out the window, playin' the music and then all the electricity went off and the music went off. And you know everybody started goin' crazy outside.

I: Yeah well, what was the first thing that went through your mind?

C: It's the end of the world, it's the end of the world. Everybody was screamin' that outside. And the neighbors said all the lights is out.

I: So you got scared? You felt frightened when the lights went out?

C: Yeah. I'm glad I was home though. I went and grabbed the babies.

I: So then what happened next?

C: And then it was on the radio and we kept talking and the lights stayed out. Everybody started breaking in stores and—

I: How do you know?

C: 'Cause I seen them and I heard them.

I: Yeah, and what did you see? That's what I'm interested in— you, your reaction to the situation. The lights went out; you were scared and then you went outside.

C: No, I didn't go right outside. I waited till later.

I: Later is about what time? Do you remember?

C: About eleven, eleven-thirty.

I: Oh, so you were late. You were an hour and a half late.

C: No. I was in the house and I . . . that's right; I went to sleep and I woke up and it was still out and I thought it was gonna be on. You know, it was still out, and that's when I went outside.

I: You know I'm trying to put everything in a stage, you know, from the time the lights went out to what happened, what you did and things like that. Right? So I'm not trying to jump, I'm just trying to take everything in a little stage. O.K., the lights went out; you were upstairs; you went to bed; you laid down to sleep because you were scared.

C: No; I went to sleep and it was a fire next door. Some boys set a fire or something, and then my mother told all of us to wake up, and I grabbed him and we went to the window, lookin' out the window, and we seen the firemen putting out the fire; and then after that was over I went downstairs for a little while. It was too dark, it was black, you couldn't see nothin' but people were flashin' lights and lightin' matches and everything, and then a bunch of boys was breaking in stores, next door, on the corner and they was getting all kinds of food and everything and me and my sister went down there and got some things.

I: From the store?

C: Uh-huh.

I: Did you think why you did it?

C: 'Cause everybody was doing it and it was free. It was right next door.

I: Do you think that you had a need to do it?

C: No. I did it for the fun of it.

I: Yeah, so it wasn't a question of need, it was a question of everybody else was doing it, so you did it?

C: Yeah.

I: What time was it about?

C: Twelve midnight.

I: O.K. Is that the only place that you went to?

C: No. Then later on that day they broke into the candy store in the middle of the block and then we was getting things from there too. And my sister was getting stuff too. Then the police was coming back and forth and trying to catch peoples.

I: What time was this now?

C: About twelve o'clock midnight; you know around that time they kept coming back and forth trying to catch people, and then the people run, then the cops come back—no, then the people come back, then they get more stuff and the cops, you know, come back to catch them.

I: Did you take part in that? Did you hit the candy store?

C: Yeah, I went down with them.

I: You got some stuff?

C: Uh-huh.

I: Did you get any, like, jewelry, radios, anything like clothes, stuff like that?

C: No, but they broke in a shoe store on the avenue, but we didn't get anything; we just heard of it, you know. I didn't go far from my door.

I: Did you know the owners?

C: Yeah.

I: The owners are white or black?

C: White.

I: O.K., how did you feel? Did you think about, did you have any feelings like, you know, hey I don't give a damn about the man who owns the place?

C: No, really. I knew he'd probably get his money back to fix the store back up. So, everybody else was getting it, ladies, grown ladies, old men and everything.

I: So you had no kind of feeling towards the owners of that store? At the time you were doing it. Let's say at the time you were doing it?

C: No, 'cause the man on the corner, I didn't like him anyway. He was too cheap, he wouldn't give nobody no credit. But when I went down there and got some things it was already messed up, the whole store was. They dun got everything anyway.

I: So what you got was just the remains more or less. Did you see anybody get caught?

C: No.

I: Did you think about if you got caught?

C: No. I didn't think they was gonna take anybody. Really, 'cause everybody was doin' it, little kids and everything.

I: Let me ask you this: how far in school did you reach? Are you still in school?

C: Uh-huh.

I: How far are you in school?

C: Eleventh grade, but I'm supposed to be in the twelfth.

I: How old are you?

C: Seventeen.

I: What's your plans for the future?

C: To be a legal secretary and a model.

I: That's good. Did you think at the time about it, when the looting was going on, about your future?

C: What? If I was gonna get caught? I didn't think I would get caught.

I: Why?

C: 'Cause it's right next door and it was too dark out there, you couldn't see anything and no cops was around at the time when I go down there.

I: So in other words you were a smart looter. You were taking things close to home. O.K., now what else? There were only two places that you hit.

C: Yeah, two places, you know, close to my home. I wasn't planning on going any place far 'cause it was so dark out there you could get lost if we just go across the street.

I: You was scared?

C: Yeah. We stayed up. When I woke back up we stayed up till about five in the morning. 'Cause my mother was up too. The next morning the lights were still out till around eight o'clock. They were still goin' gettin' stuff, they were still getting stuff from stores, and me and my sister went back down there and got some more stuff, and you could see more clearer and everything, get what you want.

I: So that's three times you went? You went down in the morning?

C: And everybody knew that the man, he didn't know nothing about it, he opens at eight o'clock, and—

I: Where does he live? Do you know?

C: No. I know he got a car and he came—

I: He don't live in this neighborhood.

C: No. He didn't know nothin' about his store. His store was wrecked, but they fixed it up now, so they were still getting stuff.

I: How about the candy store?

C: He came at seven-thirty, I think; he came early and he was shocked too.

I: Was he white or black?

C: He's Arab, I think.

I: What kind of guy is he? I mean you said you don't like the guy on the corner because he don't give credit and things like that.

C: Well, he's a real nice guy really, but they're tight too.

I: Were you ever arrested before?

C: No. For playin' hooky one time and sneakin' on the train, that's all. When I played hooky they brung me to the truant officer in Coney Island and it wasn't only me, it was my friends and all my sisters, and he wrote my name down and he asked me to find my mother's name in the phone book just in case I was lying, and he found it and he sent a truant card home. When I snuck in the train he did the same thing and gave me a card, he said if I get caught one more time I gotta go to court.

I: How old were you then?

C: Fourteen and thirteen.

I: Those were your rough years?

C: Yep.

I: Do you intend to go to college?

C: A year after I graduate. I'm gonna work for a year, then I'm gonna go to college.

I: Which one of the seven are you?

C: Well I'm the youngest of my father's kids. My stepfather, you know, the little ones are all of his kids.

I: You're the youngest of your father's. O.K., with your mother, what number are you?

C: Fourth, starting from up.

I: You're the middle child?

C: Yeah.

I: You get the best of everything.

C: No.

I: Who gets the best?

C: My littlest sister.

I: You have a little baby, though, right; what's his name again?

C: Mekeva.

I: How old is he?

C: Fourteen months.

I: What age were you when you had him?

C: Seventeen, sixteen, right. Wait, I was going on seventeen. It was last October.

I: Do you have any regrets of what happened?

C: No.

I: Did you take anything from the stores for him? Did you have that in mind when you was there?

C: Yeah, baby food and Pampers. I tried to find Pampers but they beat me to 'em.

I: When the evening came, how did you feel? Did you feel remorse, did you feel you shouldn't have done what you did or anything like that?

C: I didn't feel bad about it 'cause I wasn't really thinkin' about how they feel, but I know they was mad, but I knew they would probably get it back.

I: Why did you think that?

C: 'Cause it's too many stores. Somebody gotta get somethin' back.

I: So you felt that all along? Let's say they weren't gonna get anything back. Would you still feel—

C: Then I would feel bad about it if I would really think about it.

I: Regardless of whether he was white or black?

C: Yeah, I'm not prejudice. That have nothin' to do about it. But this man on the corner I probably wouldn't feel too bad about, 'cause he was mean. They got the cleaners too, the cleaners on the corner, but I didn't get nothin' from there.

I: You mean they took people's clothes?

C: They didn't get too much; I didn't see it, but some people were getting the clothes and everything.

I: How old is your mom?

C: Forty-one. She looks young too.

I: Where's she from, the South?

C: She was born here.

I: Did your mom go to high school too?

C: She graduated from Girls High.

I: And your pop?

C: I don't even know. I think he went to Boys High.

I: Those were the good old days when the girls were on one side and the boys were on one side. No co-eds. Your school is a co-ed school? Boys and girls all mixed together.

C: Yeah.

I: That's where you met Keith?

C: No, my friend introduced me to Keith.

I: What did your mom say when you came back upstairs with the stuff?

C: She was happy, to tell you the truth. She wasn't too mad.

I: So at least you got some stuff. You took things that you could use. What did you actually get?

C: Detergent for my mother and baby food. Big case of spinach, my sister brought that in and some regular food and everything. A little bit of everything, you know.

I: But foodstuff, all foodstuff. It make you feel good. And then you say that you didn't feel any remorse or any guilt feelings.

C: No.

I: Let me ask you this: if the lights went out again, would you do it?

C: They don't have anything left. No, I don't know what I would do.

I: What do you think you would do?

C: I won't do it like just me go down there and do it, but if they was to break in the store I'd be more careful this time 'cause I'd think they'd be ready.

I: But you would do it again if somebody broke into the store before you, right? And you saw everything was all right, you would do it again?

C: Not to the candy store 'cause I felt sorry for them afterwards. I wouldn't do it to the candy store. I'd probably do it again down there.

I: Let's say hypothetically they fixed it back up and everything, and the lights went out again; somebody broke in before you did.

C: No, I don't think I would 'cause I would be scared this time, 'cause I know they lost so much money that they would be ready, somethin' would be, you know.

I: Do you receive welfare benefits? Your sister?

C: Uh-huh.

I: Does she have a baby?

C: She's asleep.

I: Your sister's baby's asleep? How about your mom? Is she on welfare too?

C: Yes.

I: How do you feel about that? Do you feel it was a help in getting these things?

C: From the store? Yeah. I was getting it for my mother, really, and for the baby.

I: So, do you think welfare is enough to help you out?

C: I really don't think it's enough. They only give you enough to live off of. They don't give you nothin' else.

I: They give you enough to live—

C: Enough to, you know, survive off of. 'Cause my mother, she keeps extra money in the house.

I: So you all pool your resources? You pool your money, yours, your sister's. All put together and give it to your mom.

C: She gets a lot of money, but when we have it we give to her. My sister got a lot of money in the bank from when she got hit by a car, and she bought my mother the living room set and everything. When she turned eighteen she got it, and when I was working I was giving my mother my money.

I: Are you still working now?

C: In the summer I was working, but I'm gonna get the job back this summer.

I: Where were you working?

C: In a pool. A city swimming pool, give the tickets and collecting money.

I: So you were an attendant at the pool collecting money. Did you ever feel like taking some of the money?

C: Only one time I did it, but I was really scared.

I: No, I didn't ask if you did it, I asked you if you ever feel like doing it.

C: Yeah.

I: Some days when you just don't have those couple of dollars, right?

C: Yeah, that was when we took it, yeah. And, you know, we just—there's a thing you do with the tickets when you get extra money and, you know, you don't give them the ticket, and you sell the ticket over and you just keep the money. They give you the money; you can keep that money but you don't give them the ticket, and you let them go by.

I: How much is it to get in there?

C: One dollar for adults and fifty cents for kids.

I: How much did you make for yourself?

C: Ten dollars. We made twenty dollars one time, but I had to split it between me and my friend 'cause, you know, it's one that rips the tickets and I give the tickets, so we had to split it.

I: Yeah, that sounds good enough. Did you get caught?

C: No. We had three foremen, and one of the foremen he sells. He's white, too. He taught me how to do it.

I: Were all the foremen white?

C: There were two colored ones and a white one.

I: How did you feel about the entire looting? Why you did it now, the whole shebang?

C: About the blackout? How do I feel about it? I feel good about it on my behalf, but on everybody that, like, owns stores and everything, I don't feel so good about that. 'Cause after the blackout we had to go pretty far to go to the store. I don't know.

I: Tell me how you feel about it.

C: I don't really think about it that much, really.

I: You see now you just told me that you have to go all the way to the store now. But what I'm asking you is, how did you feel about the whole blackout, the whole thing? The people who were looting, did you have any feelings for them?

C: I didn't feel bad about it.

I: How about your friends?

C: After the blackout everybody was just telling everybody what they got. But I didn't really give thought to the people who lost. They got the money back, right? So nobody lost.

I: Nobody lost but you gained. Is that it?

C: I guess.

I: The looters gained.

C: Yeah, and plus they [the store owners] act so cheap all the time and, you know, I never thought anything like this would happen.

I: This is what I'm trying to ask you if you—I don't know if you had the experience, but do you feel it was right what they did, the looters, do you feel it was right what they did, right or wrong?

C: I feel it was wrong; I know it was wrong but I don't feel too bad about it 'cause that's the way some time. Maybe a long time ago [the 1965 blackout] it wasn't too many looters because you know people had jobs then and you know they didn't do too bad; the city wasn't low of money, but now it's like that. Everybody's out of a job almost, and you know everybody's down for stealin', and that's probably why there was more lootin'.

I: At least you have an opinion of the whole situation, and you felt it was because of unemployment and what else? What else you felt? What caused people to react the way they did; what caused you to react the way you did, 'cause you don't work?

C: 'Cause, you know, it don't matter to me if I don't work right now, I go to school but, like—I wanted to get some stuff for my mother and, you know, my mother didn't have too much food at the time and, you know . . .

I: O.K., let me ask you this: if she had the food at the time do you think you'd still do it?

C: I don't know. I think so but I'm not really sure.

I: But, but at the time she didn't and you saw this as an opportunity to get the food for your mother and you did. Well, I had one guy telling me that it was a blessing from heaven when the lights went off.

C: I heard a lady say that on TV. She thinks that God did that for the people in New York City, you know, 'cause of the jobs and everything.

I: Do you feel the same way?

C: Yeah, my sister heard that, I said yep. On Broadway they were breakin' in furniture stores and everything. Got TVs, they had couches on their back, and jewelry stores.

I: How did you feel about that? Did you feel that you missed out on some of that?

C: No, 'cause a lot of people got caught. About three hundred somethin' people.

I: Three thousand.

C: Three thousand? Oh Lord. See, I ain't even know about that.

I: But you didn't know that. When did you find that out?

C: The next day.

I: Yeah, but that's what friends tell you. Had you known about the jewelry store do you think that you would take part?

C: No.

I: Why not?

C: 'Cause I don't do that kind of stealin'.

I: Have you ever stole anything before and didn't get caught?

C: Like big?

I: Yeah, 'cause you didn't get caught at all.

C: Like from a store or somethin'? I can't remember. No, but I remember I did get caught one time in a department store tryin' to steal a leather coat.

I: How old were you then?

C: Fifteen, I think I was fifteen.

I: Tell me about it.

C: I was goin' to buy it, to pay on the coat really, but I didn't know they had cameras and everything in there, really; you can't see them; and I was pickin' up the coat, I was tryin' it on, and nobody was lookin', so I took the coat with me to the bathroom and I took the price tags and everything and put it in the garbage can, and they said they even know what garbage can I put it in. And they had a camera that's, I don't know, I didn't know how they find out, but then I came out. The lady in the bathroom didn't even see me and I went in the elevator, went downstairs. As soon as the elevator opened she said, come with me; then she brung me in some room. I was high at the time; I didn't care; I cared but I was laughing.

I: What were you on?

C: Started with pills.

I: O.K., so she took you into the room . . .

C: She wrote down something, asked me my name and everything, and all that. I was laughing and everything. After I seen the picture I asked her, can I have it 'cause it was in the summer, and she said it wasn't goin' on my record, it was goin' on the store record, you know, so if I ever get caught again that I gotta go to court or something, and I went home. She said I couldn't buy the coat from there. I said O.K.; I'll pay on it now 'cause I did want to buy the coat first. Then I cooled down.

I: Oh, you had others before that.

C: No, like the little stuff I was tellin' you about and the truant officer.

I: So there was the truant officer, there was the store, there was the train. That's thirteen, fourteen and fifteen, right? How about when you was sixteen?

C: Sixteen? No; I can't remember.

I: O.K., at seventeen you had the baby.

C: Yeah, sixteen, I was pregnant then, almost for that whole year.

I: Seventeen, you had the baby. Eighteen, the looting came around, the blackout.

C: No, I'm seventeen now.

I: Oh, so you had a rest when you were sixteen, a rest period. What do you think eighteen and nineteen will bring you?

C: I'm just thinkin' about the future right now, getting out of school. Ever since I got left back I been tryin' to make it back up.

I: Are you tryin' very hard?

C: Yeah.

I: Why, what makes you come around? What made you change that attitude?

C: Well, really, the way I feel, you know, ain't nothin' happenin' around here no more, really, so the only thing left to do—

I: When you say "ain't nothin' happenin'," what do you mean?

C: Like it used to be a long time ago. When we moved here, you know, a long time ago we was living across town, and that's when we knew everybody around there and we used to hang out all the time; that's when I was playing hooky a lot and that's when I got left back. Then we moved here. We know a couple of people around here, we go to parties some time but, you know, the only thing left is to go to school. But, you know, I think about, I mean I don't wanna go to school anyway.

I: You wanna get out from this kind of life?

C: Yeah. The first thing I wanna do is get my diploma and then I can take it from there.

I: How about the other ones? What are they doin'?

C: Who? My sisters?

I: Yeah, what they doin'?

C: Both of them are goin' to school now. Joan, she go to my school. We in almost the same class and Eleanor goes to a training school for her diploma 'cause she messed up too. She's nineteen and—

I: How about your brother?

C: He finished school. You know that school Albert Morrow? He graduated from there too and went and got his license permit. He doin' good. He's lookin' for a job right now 'cause he stopped workin' for about six or seven months.

I: How about the younger ones? They all goin' to school too?

C: Uh-huh.

I: There's nobody sick in the family right? Everybody's well, healthy?

C: Yep.

I: You lookin' forward to a nice Christmas and everything else. You think about Christmas?

C: But this Christmas I'm gonna be kinda broke, but as long as I get my mother a present and Keith a present, I got my presents and the baby presents. I don't care about me, but my mother she said she's gonna get me somethin'. This room is terrible. I feel like crying when I look at it sometime. We was livin' downstairs before and the landlord made us move up here, but my room down there was green, and we moved up here and they had already painted it white. I didn't want white. My mother likes white. She likes the whole house white. She say it make it look bigger.

I: You like a lot of babies?

C: Not a lot, but I think a boy and a girl, but if I had twins I would be happy.

I: How many you'd like to have?

C: Three, up to three.

I: After school, what did you say you want to do?

C: Be a legal secretary.

I: O.K., you'll do that. Do you expect to, would you like to get married?

C: No, no time soon.

I: Do you think that the economic situation will change for poor people? The crisis situation like when the blackout came, do you think things'll change?

C: Yeah, I think it will change, but no time soon. It probably is gonna change in ten more years from now.

I: What do you think is gonna bring the change?

C: It's gonna have a little bit more jobs. It's getting worse; I don't think it's getting better.

I: But you said it's gonna change. I wanna know why you think it's gonna change. What is gonna change it?

C: Somebody's gonna come along now. The President. Maybe the President.

I: How about the mayor?

C: I don't know too much about the mayor.

I: What about the governor?

C: The governor? 'Cause the job I had last summer, he gave us some jobs, Carter; what did he do? He gave a certain amount of money to the city and to bring a certain amount of jobs, right, but the way we had to get it was to go through a lottery, and you got to sign a card, you got to go to the recreation place and you got to sign a card and, you know, mail it back after you sign it, and then if they send you a letter sayin' you got it, that mean you won.

NOTES

CHAPTER I

1. Reports to the Chief of Operations, New York Police Department, by Commanding Officer of each precinct, indicated looting began almost immediately after the power failure.

2. E. L. Quarantelli and Russell R. Dynes, "Looting in Civil Disorders: An index of Social Change" *The American Behavioral Scientist* 2, no. 4 (March-April 1968): 7–10.

3. Ibid., p 9. This discussion of the stages of looting is referred to throughout this chapter.

4. All those arrested between 9:35 and 10:35 P.M. were profiled because their number was so small. Samples were used for the profiles of later groups of arrestees since there were too many of them to use entire groups.

5. Report by the President's Commission on Law Enforcement and Administration of Justice, "The Challenge of Crime in a Free Society," United States Government Printing Office, February 1967. pp. 44–6 and Chapter 3.

6. Quarantelli and Dynes, "Looting," p. 8.

7. Elliot Liebow, *Tally's Corner* (Boston: Little, Brown and Company, 1967), fn., p. 213.
8. Ibid.
9. Ibid., p. 213.

CHAPTER II

1. Ted Robert Gurr, *Why Men Rebel* (Princeton: Princeton University Press, 1970), pp. 22–58.
2. New York City Department of Planning, "Blackout Commercial Damage Survey," July 1977.
3. During the blackout period, the New York City Fire Department received 3,900 alarms; 2,223 were answered and 1,037 proved actual fires.

CHAPTER III

1. E. L. Quarantelli and Russell R. Dynes, "Looting in Civil Disorders: An Index of Social Change," *The American Behavioral Scientist* 2, no. 4 (March-April 1968): 7–8.
2. Mention of a "carnival spirit" can be found in: Dynes and Quarantelli, "What Looting in Civil Disturbances Really Means," *Trans-Action* (May 1968), p. 13; idem, "Looting," p. 9; and Edward Banfield, *The Unheavenly City Revisited* (Boston: Little, Brown and Company, 1974), p. 225.

CHAPTER IV

1. Statistics of blackout loans were provided by the Small Business Administration, Washington, D.C., September 1977.

CHAPTER V

1. A breakdown of the number of arrests made hourly was provided by the New York City Criminal Justice Agency, September 1977.
2. For a discussion of the New York Police Department regulation on use of deadly force (shooting), see p. 96.
3. Report issued by William R. Bracey, Assistant Chief, Brooklyn North Area, July 21, 1977, p. 12.
4. Report issued by Thomas Gallagher, Captain, 44th Precinct, the Bronx, July 20, 1977, p. 4.

5. Report issued by Raymond J. Abruzzi, Lieutenant, 25th Precinct, East Harlem, July 20, 1977, p. 4.

6. Reports describing the events during the blackout were issued by each precinct to the Police Department's Chief of Operations. References to tactics used and arrests made that appear in this chapter are from the individual precinct reports.

7. "Critique of Incident-Blackout 1977," issued by Charles T. Mancuso, Lieutenant, Brooklyn North Area Task Force, July 19, 1977, p. 2.

8. The precincts used were the 24th and 28th in Manhattan, the 46th and 48th in the Bronx, and the 67th and 81st in Brooklyn.

9. The precincts used were the 7th, 23rd, 24th, 26th, 28th and 30th in Manhattan; the 67th, 72nd and 81st in Brooklyn; the 40th and 48th in the Bronx.

10. Report issued by James B. Meehan, Deputy Chief, Staten Island Area, July 21, 1977, p. 5.

11. Report issued by Raymond J. McDermott, Assistant Chief, Bronx Field Services Area, July 21, 1977.

12. Report, Brooklyn North Area, p. 16.

13. Report, 25th Precinct, p. 3.

14. Report issued by Brian F. Lavin, Captain in Command, 48th Precinct, the Bronx, July 19, 1977, p. 6.

15. For a discussion of the role of the National Guard see: Joseph Martin and Paul Meskil, "Costly Right Guard Protection was Shelved in Dark," *Daily News*, July 25, 1977, p. 3, and Thomas Poster, "Duryea Raps Governor for Failure to Call Guard in Blackout," *Daily News*, August 3, 1977, p. 49.

16. Dennis Wenger, "The Reluctant Army: The Functioning of Police Departments during Civil Disorders," *The American Behavioral Scientist* 16, no. 3 (January-February 1973): 326–42.

17. See George Kelling et al., *The Kansas City Preventive Patrol Experiment: A Summary Report:* (Washington, D.C., Police Foundation, 1974); James Levine, "The Ineffectiveness of Adding Police to Prevent Crime," *Public Policy* 23, no. 4 (Fall 1975): 523–45.

CHAPTER VI

1. For a discussion of the community's impact on police behavior see James Q. Wilson, *Varieties of Police Behavior* (New York: Atheneum, 1973), chapter 8.

2. Peter Greenwood, *An Analysis of the Apprehension Activities of the New York City Police Department* (New York: The New York City Rand Institute, 1970), pp. 37–9.

3. James P. Levine, "The Ineffectiveness of Adding Police to Prevent Crime," *Public Policy* 23, no. 4 (Fall 1975): 523–45.

CHAPTER VII

1. Five-part series, *New York Times*, 24–8 August 1977, pp.
2. "50% of 176 Cited in Looting Held Full-Time Jobs," *New York Times*, 9 August 1977, p. 34.
3. Stewart Ain, "Find Looters Not Hungry," *Daily News*, 9 August 1977, p. 5.
4. New York City Criminal Justice Agency, "A Demographic Profile of Defendants Arrested in the New York City Blackout: A Preliminary Report," August 1977, pp. 1–2.
5. Molly Ivins, "Legal Aid Society May Turn Out to be Unlikely Victim of Blackout," *New York Times*, 27 July 1977, p. 42.
6. Ain, "Looters Not Hungry."
7. Ibid.
8. Steven R. Weisman, "City Constructs Statistical Profile in Looting Cases," *New York Times*, 14 August 1977, p. 1.
9. Robert Crane, "Looting Suspects Had Stable Roots: Study," *Daily News*, 14 August 1977, p. 33.

CHAPTER VIII

1. Merrill Sheils et al., "Blackout Justice," *Newsweek*, 1 August 1977, pp. 67–8.
2. *Report of the Select Committee on Criminal Justice Emergency Preparedness*, October 31, 1977.
3. Ibid.
4. The number of arrests made in each borough were: Manhattan: 836; Bronx: 961; Brooklyn: 1,088; Queens: 191.
5. *Select Committee on Criminal Justice*, p. 4.
6. New York State Office of Court Administration, New York, July 21, 1977, p. 3.
7. *Select Committee on Criminal Justice*, p. 8.
8. Ibid., pp. 4, 9.
9. "A Demographic Profile of Defendants Arrested in the New York City Blackout: A Preliminary Report," New York City Criminal Justice Agency, August 1977.
10. Sheils, "Blackout Justice," p. 68.
11. "Most Looting Suspects Are Out of Jail," *New York Post*, 29 July 1977, p. 3.
12. Alan Bent and Ralph Rossum, *Police, Criminal Justice and the Community*
13. New York City Department of Criminal Justice.
14. New York City Criminal Justice Agency, Op. Cit. Summary Findings IV 7 & 8.

15. Sheils, "Blackout Justice," p. 68.
16. *Select Committee on Criminal Justice,* Appendix C, p. 27.
17. "Most Looting Suspects," p. 3.
18. *The New York Times,* July 13, 1978.

CHAPTER IX

1. Statistics on neighborhood demography were provided by the New York City Department of City Planning, May 1977.
2. Study conducted by the Manhattan Valley Development Corporation.
3. Mills, "Panic in Needle Park," *Life Magazine,* 26 February 1965.
4. New York City Department of City Planning, *Upper West Side Development,* 1958.
5. Data on number and location of looted stores compiled by the Department of City Planning, July 1977. See tables in Chapter II.
6. Names and addresses of arrestees provided in precinct reports.
7. Precinct reports included addresses at which arrests were made.
8. Paul Delaney, "Bushwick: Nothing to Lose," *New York Times,* 24 July 1977.
9. Crime statistics cited in this chapter are compiled by the New York City Police Department. See *Statistical Report: Complaints and Arrests.*
10. New York City Fire Department, *Annual Statistics.*

CHAPTER X

1. Data on financing, employment and housing were provided by Public Relations Office, Bedford Stuyvesant Restoration Corporation.
2. See "Carter to New York: I'm Off to Yazoo City," *Philadelphia Inquirer,* 21 July 1977, p. 10A.
3. Combined reports of New York City Department of Planning and New York City Police Department on damaged and looted stores.

CHAPTER XI

1. Russell Dynes and E. L. Quarantelli, "What Looting in Civil Disturbances Really Means," *Trans-Action* (May 1968), p 9.
2. Edward C. Banfield, *The Unheavenly City Revisited* (Boston: Little, Brown and Company, 1974).
3. Dynes and Quarantelli, "Looting in Civil Disturbances," p. 10.
4. Frances Fox Piven and Richard A. Cloward, *Poor People's Movements* (New York: Pantheon, 1977), p. 49.

5. Irving Bernstein, *The Lean Years: A History of the American Worker 1920–1933* (Boston: Houghton Mifflin Co., 1960), p. 422.

6. Dynes and Quarantelli, "Looting in Civil Disorders: An Index of Social Change," *The American Behavioral Scientist* 2, no. 4 (March-April 1968): 9.

7. Ted Robert Gurr, *Why Men Rebel* (Princeton: Princeton University Press, 1970), pp. 22–58.

8. Ibid., p. 48.

9. See Norman R. C. Cohn, *The Pursuit of the Millenium*, 2nd rev. ed. (New York: Harper & Row, 1960), quoted in Gurr.

10. E. J. Hobsbawm, *Social Bandits and Primitive Rebels: Studies in Archaic Forms of Social Movement in the 19th and 20th Centuries* (Glencoe: The Free Press, 1959), p. 23–4, quoted in Gurr.

11. Gurr, pp. 48–9.

12. Ibid., p. 50.

13. Ibid., p. 52. See James C. Davies, "Toward a Theory of Revolution," *American Sociological Review*, 27 (February 1962), pp. 5–19.

14. Allan D. Grimshaw, "Actions of Police and Military in American Race Riots," *Phylon* (Fall, 1963).

15. Stanley Lieberson and Arnold Silverman, "The Precipitants and Underlying Conditions of Race Riots," *American Sociological Review* 30 (December 1965), pp. 887–98.

16. Abraham Miller et al., "The J-Curve Theory and the Black Urban Riots," *The American Political Science Review*, 71 (September 1977) pp. 964–82.

17. *Report of the National Advisory Commission on Civil Disorders* (New York: Bantam Books, 1968), p. 10.

18. Ibid., p. 10.

19. Robert M. Fogelson and Robert B. Hill, "Who Riots? A Study of Participation in the 1967 Riots," *Supplemental Studies for the National Advisory Commission on Civil Disorders* (Washington, D.C.: United States Government Printing Office, July 1968), pp. 241–43.

20. Banfield, *Unheavenly City*, p. 212.

21. *Advisory Commission on Civil Disorders*, pp. 109–12.

CHAPTER XII

1. Herbert Gutman, "As for the '02 Kosher-Food Rioters," *New York Times* Op-Ed page, 21 July 1977.

2. Diane Ravitch, "Not Always a Matter of Justice," *New York Times* Op-Ed page, 27 July 1977.

3. Midge Decter, "Looting and Liberal Racism," *Commentary*, September 1977.

4. Henry Bienen, *Violence and Social Change* (Chicago: University of Chicago Press, 1968).

5. Michael Lipsky and David Olsen, "The Processing of Racial Crisis in America," *Politics and Society* 6, no. 1 (1976).

BIBLIOGRAPHY

Newspaper and Magazine Articles

Ain, Stewart. "Finds Looters Not Hungry." *Daily News*, 9 August 1977, p. 5

Asbury, Edith Evans. "Carey Allots $1 million from State to Hire 2,000 for Blackout Cleanup." *New York Times*, 7 July 1977, p. B4.

Barmash, Isadore. "Stores Anxious About Insurance." *New York Times*, 16 July 1977.

Beker, Brian. "West Siders Meet About Looting." *Our Town*, 29 July 1977.

"Blackout: New Paralysis, New Symptoms: Much Uglier." *New York Times*, 17 July 1977.

Breasted, Mary. "Carey and President Scored on Blackout." *New York Times*, 3 August 1977, p. A15.

Carmody, Deidre. "Ravaged Slums Facing A Future Uncertainty." *New York Times*, 16 July 1977, p. Al.

Carroll, Robert. "Brooklyn Hardest Hit in Blackout." *Daily News*, 24 July 1977, pp. 3,

"Catharsis Time again at Con Ed." Time Magazine, 25 July 1977, pp. 46–7.

Cockburn, Alexander, et al. "Conned Again: God Geta A Bum Rap." *Village Voice*, 25 July 1977, pp. 1,

Coombs, Orde. "The trashing of Le Mans: The New Civil War Begins." *New York Magazine*, 8 August 1977, pp. 43–5.

Crittenden, Ann. "Case of the Black Entrepreneur." *New York Times*, 31 July 1977, p. 1.

Cummings, Judith. "Store-Pillaging Unchecked in Two Brooklyn Sections." *New York Times*, 15 July 1977.

Daly, Michael, et al. "Here Comes the Neighborhood." *Village Voice*, 25 July 1977.

Delany, Paul. "Bushwick: Nothing to Lose." *New York Times*, 24 July 1977.

Dionne, E. J., Jr. "Owner of A Looted Store in Bronx Exchanges Words with the Mayor." *New York Times*, 17 July 1977.

Edmonds, Richard. "Luce: Con Edison Not Responsible for Fires, Looting." *Daily News*, 25 August 1977, p. 3.

Elliott, Osborn. "Where Looters Fled, Volunteers Tough it Out." *Daily News*, 29 July 1977, p. 28.

Fallon, Beth. "Hope, Fear on Street Where They Live." *Daily News*, 10 August 1977, p. 32.

Fitzgerald, Owen. "They Get 1st Grants to Open for Business." *Daily News*, 27 July 1977, p. 3.

———. "Few Victims of Blackout Ask Grants." *Daily News*, 29 July 1977, p. 3.

———. "Volunteers Are Batting For Victims of Looting." *Daily News*, 31 July 1977, p. 10.

Flanagan, William. "Where Was Luce When The Lights Went Out." *New York Magazine*, 1 August 1977, p. 32.

Fowler, Glenn. "Suppliers Expecting Big Profits In Power Failure Are Proved Wrong." *New York Times*, 24 July 1977, p. 32.

Gelinz, Robert. "Aid Is Due In Wake of Looting." *Daily News*, 25 July 1977.

Goldstein, Tom. "After The Blackout, Justice Goes By the Book." *New York Times*, 18 July 1977.

Gometz, Dalia. "Fifth Ave. Merchants Set Losses In Thousands." *Home Reporter and Sunset News*, 22 July 1977.

Gooding, Richard, et al. "Con Ed Explains Its Goof." *New York Post*, 27 July 1977, p. 12.

Gottlieb, Martin, et al. "Our Dying Neighborhoods": Five-Part Series. *Daily News*, 1–5 August 1977.

Griffin, Amy. "BRAVO Beset By Calls During Blackout Here." *Home Reporter*, 22 July 1977, p. 4.

Gupte, Pranay. "A Trial By Heat in New York Jails." New York Times.

————. "White House Grants $11.3 Million In Aid for Blackout Losses." *New York Times*, 24 July 1977.

————. "U.S. Considers More Assistance To New York For Blackout Losses," *New York Times*, 25 July 1966.

————. "Bushwick Block Seeking Light After Enduring Blackout." *New York Times*, 12 August 1977, p. B1.

Herbert, Bob. "Feds Find Con Ed Bungled Blackout." *Daily News*, 30 July 1977, p. 3.

Ireland, Doug. "The Politics of Darkness." *New York Magazine*, 1 August 1977, pp. 8–9.

Jensen, Michael. "Con Ed's Own Power Is Also Limited." *New York Times*, 24 July 1977, p. 7.

Kappstatter, Bob. "TA Official Kept Cool In Blackout." *Daily News*, 24 July 1977.

Kihss, Peter. "Theft-Damage Cost in Blackout Put at $135 Million." *New York Times*, 22 July 1977, p. A2.

Koshetz, Charles. "Looter-Damaged Computer Points Up Big Vulnerability." *New York Post*, 8 August 1977, p. 48.

Lawrence, Steve, and Robert Carroll. "Claims Too Much Juice Made Con Ed Slip." *Daily News*, 27 July 1977, p. 17.

Leahy, Jack. "East New York Sounds Alarm To Prevent Another Bushwick." *Daily News*, 11 August 1977, p. K2.

Lee, Vincent, Peter McLaughlin, and Paul Meskil. "Scoppetta: Trials for Less Than 10% in Blackout." *Daily News*, 27 July 1977, p. 16.

Lieberman, Mark. "Pay $1.2 M to Looted Merchants." *Daily News*, 5 August 1977, p. 20.

Llewellyn, J. Bryce, and Adam Walinsky. "Blackout Lessons." *New York Times*, 31 July 1977.

Lynn, Frank. "Survey Shows New Yorkers Link Lootings to Thieving, Not Protest." *New York Times*, 27 August 1977, pp. 1.

Martin, Joseph, and Paul Meskil. "Costly Right Guard Protection Was Shelved in Dark." *Daily News*, 25 July 1977, pp. 3.

Mason, Bryant. "A Business Struggles to Pick Up the Pieces." *Daily News*, 24 July 1977, p. B1.

————. "Looted Biz Eyes Haven In Bed-Stuy Plaza." *Daily News*, 7 August 1977, p. K1.

————. "Blackout Looting Charge Faces Wright's Brother." *Daily News*, 23 August 1977, p. 8.

McFadden, Robert D. "New York Power Restored." *New York Times*, 15 July 1977, p. Al.

Miele, Alfred. "Blackout '77 Spawns Retired Cops Stand-By Plan." *Daily News*, 30 July 1977, p. 8.

"Misdirected Fire." Editorial. *Daily News*, 26 July 1977, p. 33.

"Night of Terror." *Time Magazine*, 25 July 1977, pp. 12–22.

Otey, Sara M. "Blackout '77: Residents Frolic, Merchants Fret." *Home Reporter and Sunset News*, 22 July 1977, p. 2.

Pace, Eric. "A Grim Game of Cat and Mouse in Tour of East Harlem." *New York Times*, 15 July 1977, p. A5.

"Picking Up the Pieces." *Newsweek*, 1 July 1977, pp. 560,

Plate, Thomas. "Why The Cops Didn't Shoot." *New York Magazine*, 1 August 1977, pp. 29–31.

Poster, Thomas. "City to Get $11.35M in Looting Aid. *Daily News*, 24 July 1977, pp 3T.

———. "Duryea Raps Gov. For Failure To Call Guard in Blackout." *Daily News*, 3 August 1977, p. 49.

Raab, Selwyn. "Ravage Continues Far Into Day; Gunfire And Bottles Beset Police." *New York Times*, 15 July 1977, p. Al.

Ravitch, Diane. "Not Always A Matter of Justice." *New York Times*, 27 July 1977, p. A19.

Reel, William. "Praying For Green Lights In Bushwick." *Daily News*, 17 August 1977, p. 42.

Saxon, Wolfgang. "Con Ed Acts To Cut Cause of Blackouts." *New York Times*, 17 July 1977, p. Al.

"S.B.A. Halves Blackout Loan Rate." News Briefs. *Daily News*, 11 August 1977, p. 40.

Schmetterer, Jerry. "Lights Are On Again For a Small Bizman." *Daily News*, 4 August 1977, p. BKL 1.

Schoen, Elin. "Twenty Bright Ideas For The Next Blackout." *New York Magazine*, 1 August 1977, pp. 35–6.

Severo, Richard. "Two Blackouts And a World Of Difference." *New York Times*, 16 July 1977, p.

Sheppard, Joan. "Group Paves The Way For Flatbush Ave. Renewal." *Daily News*, 31 July 1977, p. K1.

———. "Fire-Bombed Bushwick Plans Protest." *Daily News*, 4 August 1977, p. B6.

———. "Bushwick Is Still Slow In Cleaning Streets, But It's a Litter Better." *Daily News*, 23 August 1977, p. BKL 1.

Simpson, Janice, and Derek Reveron. "Own Your Own Apartment House—For The Price of A Second-Hand Car." *New York Post*, 1 August 1977, pp. 28–9.

Slagle, Alton. "They Call A Gas Can An 'Overnight Bag.'" *Daily News*, 2 August 1977, pp. T7.

Stathos, Harry, et al. "Urge Speedy Loot Insurance Payoffs." *Daily News*, 26 July 1977, p. 3.

Sullivan, Walter. "Con Ed Delay Cited As a Probable Cause." *New York Times*, 16 July 1977, p. Al.

"The Blackout: Counting Losses In The Rubble." *Time Magazine*, 1 August 1977, pp. 14,

"The Tragedy of Bushwick." Editorial. *Daily News*, 7 August 1977.

Treaster, Joseph B. "Blackout Arrests Swamp City's Criminal Justice System." *New York Times*, 15 July 1977, p. Al.

"U.S. Shortchanges N.Y. Region." *New York Post*, 8 August 1977, p. 50.

Vanzi, Cass, and Richard Esmonds. "Luce and Cops Strike Sparks Over Cause of Blackout Looting." *Daily News*, 26 July 1977, p. 3.

Van Gelden, Lawrence. "Some Civilians Assist Police—'65 Blackout Peaceful in Contrast." *New York Times*, 14 July 1977, p. 1.

Wald, Matthew. "Looting Cases Persist As a Problem." *New York Times*, 21 July 1977.

Weiss, Murray, "Utica Ave. Bizmen Demand City Aid." *Daily News*, 7 August 1977, p. K1.

"Where Were Harlem Police." *N.Y. Amsterdam News*, 30 July 1977, pp. A1.

"When The News Tickers Fell Silent." *Time Magazine*, 25 July 1977, p. 43.

White, David F. "A Glimpse At Bushwick's Broadway After the Looting." *New York Times*, 16 July 1977, p. Al.

"Who Gets The Blame." *New York Magazine*, 1 August 1977, pp. 33–4.

"Why The Lights Went Out." *Time Magazine*, 25 July 1977, pp. 24–5.

Wieghart, James, and Bruce Drake. "U.S. Blackout Report Cites 'Obvious Flaws' In Con Ed's System." *Daily News*, 4 August 1977, p. 2.

Books and Journal Articles

American Newspaper Publishers Association. *Reporting The Detroit Riot*. April 1968.

Anderson, William A., et al. *"Urban Counterrioters."* Reprint #87. Reprinted from *Transaction: Social Science and Modern Society*, March-April 1974, pp. 50–55. Disaster Research Center, The Ohio State University.

Bell, Harold K. *Business As Usual. The Cockroach Approach*. Graduate School of Architecture and Planning, Columbia University, November 1977.

Bernstein, Irving. *The Lean Years: A History of The American Worker 1920–1933*. Boston: Houghton Mifflin Co., 1960.

———. *The Turbulent Years: A History Of The American Worker 1933–1941*. Boston: Houghton Mifflin Co., 1970.

Bienen, Henry. *Violence and Social Changes. A Review of Current*

Literature. The Adlai Stevenson Institute of International Affairs. Chicago: University of Chicago Press, 1968.

Bondarin, Arley. *New York City's Population—1974: Socioeconomic Characteristics From The Current Population Survey.* New York: Center for New York City Affairs, New School for Social Research, April 1976.

Brown, Roscoe C., Jr. *The Social And Economic Roots Of The Blackout 'Disturbances'."* 1973, 1974, 1975.

Christmas, June J. *Private Initiatives And The Revitalization Of Communities.* Keynote Address, Council on Foundation, 6 May 1977.

Conot, Robert. *Rivers of Blood, Years of Darkness.* New York: Bantam Books, Inc., 1967.

Critchley, T. A. *The Conquest of Violence: Order and Liberty In Britain.* New York: Schocken Books Inc., 1970.

DeCicco, Paul R. "What To Do With Existing Row-Frame Residential Buildings." *Fire Journal,* November 1976, pp. 23.

Department of City Planning, City of New York. *Estimated Measurable Population For Health Areas in New York City. July 1, 1975.* May 1977.

———. *Preliminary Findings: Blackout Commercial Damage Survey.* July 1977.

———. *Social Profile Human Resource District 12.* November 1960.

Department of Social Services, City of New York. *Monthly Statistical Report.* June 1971; December 1971; June 1972; December 1972.

Department of Welfare, City of New York. *Monthly Statistical Report.* June 1966; December 1966.

Disaster Research Center. *Publications Part A.* Columbus: The Ohio State University, September 1977.

Division of Criminal Justice Services, State of New York. *Findings of Task Force to Study Blackout Related Defendants.* August 1977.

Dynes, Russell R., and E. L. Quarantelli. *Helping Behavior in Large Scale Disasters: A Social Organizational Approach.* Reprint #90. Reprinted from *Voluntary Action Research,* edited by Jacqueline Macauley and David Horton Smith, Lexington, Mass.: Lexington Books, 1975.

———. *Organization As Victim In Mass Civil Disturbances.* Reprint #47. Reprinted from *Issues In Criminology,* summer 1970, pp. 181–93. Disaster Research Center, The Ohio State University.

———. "What Looting In Civil Disturbances Really Means." *Trans-Action,* May 1968, pp. 9–14.

Feagin, Joe R., and Harlan Hahn. *Ghetto Revolts. The Politics of Violence in American Cities.* New York: Macmillan Co., 1973.

Fire Department, City of New York. *Annual Statistics.* 1970–1973.

Foundation For Child Development. "State of The Child: New York City." April 1976.

Goering, John M., and Edward T. Rogowsky. *Solomon's Choice: The Dilemma of Neighborhood, Race and Stability.* Urban Analysis Center and the Doctoral Program In Sociology. New York: Graduate School and University Center, City University of New York, 1977.

Gurr, Ted Robert. *Why Men Rebel*. Princeton, N.J.: Princeton University Press, 1970.

Harlem Task Force. *A Profile Of The Harlem Area*. December 1973.

Hayden, Tom. *Rebellion in Newark: Official Violence And Ghetto Response*. New York: Vintage Books, 1967.

Human Resources Administration, City of New York. *Monthly Statistical Report*. June 1973; December 1973; June 1974; December 1974; June 1975; December 1975; June 1976; December 1976; May 1977.

———. Department of Social Services. *Office of Special Housing Services. New York City Hotel Study*. March 1975.

———. *A Demographic Profile Of New York City*. September 1973.

Human Resources District No. 13. *The Plan For Community Social Services: East* New York. 7 March 1972. Revised 13 March 1972.

Hummel, Ralph P. *Command Change And Police Protest*. New York: Urbia Associates, 1975.

Israel, Joachim. *Alienation: From Mark To Modern Sociology*. Boston: Allyn and Bacon, Inc., 1971.

Joint Center For Political Studies. Harrington J. Bryce, ed. *Black Crime: A Police View*. Police Foundation. Law Enforcement Assistance. [Administration 1977.]

Kelly, Rita Mae. *Increasing Community Influence Over Police*. Paper delivered at 1972 Annual Meeting of the American Political Science Association, September 5–19.

Liebow, Elliot. *Tally's Corner. A Study of Negro Streetcorner Men*. Boston: Little, Brown and Co., 1967.

Lipsky, Michael, and David Olson. "The Processing of Racial in America." *Politics and Society*. 1976, pp. 79–103

Miller, Abraham H., et al. "The J-Curve and The Black Urban Riots." *The American Political Science Review*. September 1977, pp. 964–82.

Mitchell, J. Paul, ed. *Race Riots In Black and White*. Englewood Cliffs, N.J.: Prentice-Hall, Inc., 1970.

New York City Criminal Justice Agency. *A Demographic Profile of Defendants Arrested In The New York City Blackout: A Preliminary Report*. August 1977.

New York City Planning Commission. *Community Planning District Profiles: Part I—Population and Housing; Part II—Socio-Economic Characteristics*. September 1974.

———. *Community School District Profiles: Socio-Economic Characteristics*. July 1974.

———. *New Dwelling Units Completed 1973–1974; New York City Community Planning Districts*. June 1975.

————. *Community Planning Handbook. Brooklyn Community Planning District 4.* September 1973.

————. *Community Planning Handbook. Bronx Community Planning District 5.* September 1973.

————. *Sectional Maps of New York City.* January 1975.

New York State Office of Court Administration. Press Release. 21 July 1977.

Nocerino, Kathryn. *The Home Relief Singles Caseload in New York City—December 1975.* PA Study E1. New York: Office of Research and Program Evaluation. Human Resources Administration. January 1977.

Office of Public Affairs. *New York City Community Corporation Areas (Poverty Areas).* March 1972.

Ostrom, Elinor, and Gordon Whitaker. *Black Citizens and the Police: Some Effects of Community Control.* Paper delivered at 1971 Annual Meeting of the American Political Science Association. September 7–11.

Piven, Frances Fox. "The Social Structuring of Political Protest." *Politics and Society.* 6. 297–326.

————, and Richard A. Cloward. *Regulating The Poor: The Functions of Public Welfare.* New York: Vintage Books, 1971.

Police Department, City of New York. *Statistical Report: Complaints And Arrests—1972, 1974–1977.* Office of Management Analysis, Crime Analysis Section.

Quarantelli, E. L., and Russell Dynes. *Property Norms and Looting: Their Pattern In Community Crisis.* Reprint #46. Disaster Research Center, The Ohio State University, 1968.

————. "Looting in Civil Disorders: An Index of Social Change." *The American Behavioral Scientist*, March-April 1968, pp. 7–10.

————. *Social Aspects of Disasters And Their Relevance To Pre-Disaster Planning.* Reprint #103. Disaster Research Center, The Ohio State University. *Disasters.* 1: 98–107.

Ross, Thomas, ed. *Violence In America. A Historical And Contemporary Reader.* New York: Vintage Books, 1970.

Sternlieb, George, and James W. Hughes. *Housing and Economic Reality: New York City 1976.* Center for Urban Policy Research, Rutgers—The State University of New Jersey.

Supplemental Studies For the National Advisory Commission on Civil Disorders. Washington, D.C., United States Government Printing Office, July 1968.

Toplin, Robert Brent. *Unchallenged Violence: An American Ordeal.* Westport, Conn.: Greenwood Press, 1975.

U.S. Riot Commission Report. *Report of The National Advisory Commission on Civil Disorders.* New York: Bantam Books, 1968.

Vera Institute of Justice. *Felony Arrests: Their Prosecution and Disposition In New York City's Courts.* 1977.

Walker, James. *Police And The Community: Preventive Medicine Or Intensive Care?* Paper delivered at the 1972 Annual Meeting of the American Political Science Association, September 5–9.

Wilson, James Q. *Varieties of Police Behavior. The Management of Law and Order in Eight Communities.* New York: Atheneum, 1973.

INDEX